Sugarball

Sugarball

• • • • • • • • • • •

THE AMERICAN GAME, THE DOMINICAN DREAM

ALAN M. KLEIN

YALE UNIVERSITY PRESS   NEW HAVEN & LONDON

Published with assistance from the
Louis Stern Memorial Fund.

Designed by Richard Hendel.
Set in Electra type by G&S Typesetters,
Austin, Texas.
Printed in the United States of America
by Vail-Ballou Press, Binghamton,
New York.

Library of Congress Cataloging-in-Publication Data

Klein, Alan M., 1946–
    Sugarball: the American game, the Dominican dream / Alan M. Klein.
        p.   cm.
    Includes bibliographical references and index.
    ISBN 0-300-04873-4 (alk. paper)
        1. Baseball—Social aspects— Dominican Republic.   2. Baseball—
    Political aspects—Dominican Republic.   I. Title.
    GV863.29.A1D655   1991
    796.357'097293—dc20

90-45953
CIP

The paper in this book meets the
guidelines for permanence and durability
of the Committee on Production

Guidelines for Book Longevity of the
Council on Library Resources.

10 9 8 7 6 5 4 3 2 1

For my parents,

JOSEPH *&* SONIA KLEIN,

who after suffering the

horrors of the concentration

camps have still been able

to affirm life and give me

the support and courage

to go on with mine

Contents

Preface

This study of baseball in the Dominican Republic was carried out over two years between 1987 and 1989, during which I made four trips to the Dominican Republic, each lasting four to six weeks. During these trips I focused my attention on the academies and Quisqueya Stadium, conducted a wide range of interviews and surveys, and made many observations. I also formed and conducted an English class at the Los Angeles Dodgers' academy (Campo Las Palmas). Back in the United States I continued to interview Dominicans who played in their country during the 1940s and 1950s. Some of my methodology and survey materials are given in the appendix.

There are a number of people and organizations I would like to thank for making this book possible. Chief among them is the Los Angeles Dodgers organization and its executive vice president, Fred Claire, who, continuing the Dodger tradition of progressive and forward-looking management, gave me access to the club's operations and encouraged me throughout my work. In looking as closely as I did at the Dodgers' operations in the Dominican Republic I was bound to unearth some shortcomings, but I also discovered the lengths to which the Dodgers are willing to go to improve their operations. The same cannot be said of most of the other franchises in the country.

My book would never have moved along without the help of my assistant, Aida Tavarez Ruiz. She wore many hats: translator in the earliest phases of my work, survey researcher, language teacher in the baseball academy, and liaison between others and me. Jeff Sperber, a project photographer and family friend, was instrumental to me both as an aide during one of my stays and as a photographer.

What made my work so pleasurable were the people both in and out of baseball with whom I came in regular contact. Of the baseball family in the Dominican Republic, several members deserve special mention. Cesarín Gerónimo, president of the Dominican players' association FENAPEPRO, was extremely generous with his time, insights, and introductions to others. Cúqui Córdova, the foremost baseball historian in the Dominican Republic, regaled me with stories of baseball traditions and allowed me to use his archives. Chico Conton and Austin Jacobo were indispensable in helping me to write about baseball played in the refineries. Ed McNamara, a transplanted American, was most helpful in getting me introductions and at times served as an independent check on various data. Gil and Helen Rosenthal supported me from the first days of my research, giving freely of home and hospitality. But most important to all my work was Ralph Avila, director of Campo Las Palmas and the head of scouting in Latin America for the Los Angeles Dodgers. From our first encounter he demonstrated his acumen not only for baseball but in a wide range of fields. His naturally analytical mind and capacity for critical thinking proved invaluable to me. Avila was generous with his time and patience and with his wife, Gloria, gave me some very badly needed home-cooked meals as well.

I embarked on my study seeking a change in my research focus. As a Native American specialist who had recently turned to sports sociology, I sought to shift toward Latin American studies. As a novice I got lukewarm encouragement from many, but there were also those who gave me wholehearted support and I thank them especially. Stateside, I want to thank my parents, Joseph and Sonia Klein, for their generous financial support and their belief in me. Northeastern University provided me with a grant for one of my trips and, more important, with a set of colleagues who are supportive and helpful. Two friends played key roles. Milton Jamail, a fellow baseball researcher, and Norberto James, a Dominican poet, offered me their time and expertise. My thanks go to Christine Gailey and Craig Reinerman for reading earlier drafts of some of this work and to Mary Mello for help in editing this manuscript. At Yale University Press Ellen Graham saw this work as worthwhile and encouraged me, while Fred Kameny saw it through the editorial process; to both I am grateful. Finally, thanks to Lindy Laub, who unwittingly served as an impetus for this book and, shocked to find that she had done so, helped me along. My son, Jed, gave me several keen insights as well and said I would not remember him in the acknowledgments. To all these people my thanks for the kind words that nurtured and guided me.

Baseball is not a form of warfare or aggression, but it does have at least one unique kind of confrontation, a test of individual worth unlike any other found in sport or society. When a player goes to bat he leaves behind his teammates in the dugout and ventures out alone to face his enemies. Armed only with a bat, he sees the entire opposition arrayed in front of him. It is a difficult situation in which the batter usually fails: even the best hitters succeed only about one time in three. The worst humiliation for a batter is to be struck out, for then he has to walk back to his teammates, muttering to himself, while the other team gleefully throws around the ball. The tensions between a batter who has two strikes against him and the opposing pitcher are a metaphor for the political and cultural tensions described in this book.

Introduction

*If you ask any Dominican what he is proudest of, he will read
you a list of ballplayers. This country doesn't have much, but we
know we are the best in the world at one thing [baseball]. That's
not bragging, because it's true. And we plan to continue being
the best in the world at it.*
   —*Manuel Mota of the Dominican Republic, former outfielder
   for the Los Angeles Dodgers*

To the average Dominican, baseball is a major source of cultural pride. The country's identification with the game is deep and the
signs are pervasive: "From the moment you're born in San Pedro [de
Macorís]—at least if you're a boy—you're exposed to baseball. When
you're born, the hospital puts a pink ribbon in your crib if you're a girl,
and a baseball glove if you're a boy." [1] To any of the tens of thousands of
gifted players in the Dominican Republic, *pelota* (baseball) is an opportunity to escape a life of poverty; while to the major league franchises
there, the country is a seemingly endless source of cheap and genuine
talent. In the Dominican Republic baseball has become much more
than a game, even more than a national pastime: it is a crucial arena of
intercultural relations, in which significance attaches to everything
about the game, its symbols, and its players. In the Dominican Republic baseball has a place all out of proportion to the normal one of
sport in society. There is nothing comparable to it in the United States,
nothing as central, as dearly held as baseball is for Dominicans. Americans may love the game of baseball as much as Dominicans do, but
they do not need it as much. For Dominicans baseball is a wide-ranging
set of symbols: every turn at bat is a candle of hope, every swing is the
wave of a banner, the sweeping arc of a sword.
   There are a number of reasons to study baseball in the Dominican
Republic, but foremost is the need to explain its exaggerated importance. In this book I focus on the conflict between the United States,
which originated the game of baseball and continues to control it, and
the Dominican Republic, which having adopted the North American   1

sport refashioned it to Dominican ends and now strives to keep it its own. Major league clubs and their Dominican partners and affiliates operate very much like other powerful economic and cultural interests of the United States in the third world. They promote inferiority and subordination in the face of powerful foreigners. The special role that American popular culture plays in promoting the presence of the United States throughout the world has been clear ever since the publication of *How to Read Donald Duck* (1975) by Ariel Dorfman and Armand Mattelart. But although there have been many studies of the impact of the political, economic, and military presence of the United States in the third world, relatively few have examined the impact of its cultural presence.

Baseball is particularly well suited to a study of the cultural role of the United States in the Dominican Republic. Because of widespread poverty there are few economic options open to men. The work force in the Dominican Republic is unskilled and increasingly shifting from agricultural labor to makeshift urban labor. Displaced farmers flood the cities, where they find menial jobs in tourism and construction, or no jobs at all. Grueling, arduous, and despised though it is, cutting cane continues to be the most easily obtained employment in the country. It is also the future many men fear for themselves if baseball should fail them, all of which further elevates the status of baseball in the Dominican Republic.

The Dominican Republic has produced more professional and major league baseball players than any country apart from the United States, and proportionately more players than any country including the United States. Journalists have marveled at the omnipresence of the sport in the Dominican Republic, at the intensity with which young men pursue baseball to the exclusion of other things. This book documents the sport's hallowed position in Dominican society, as well as the extent and consequences of its success.

American major league teams operating in the Dominican Republic channel the direction the sport takes. These teams operate much like other large corporations in the third world, with one exception: whereas giants such as Falconbridge and GTE are resented, major league teams are largely supported. Because it does not provoke the ambivalence or outright hostility that other American interests do, popular culture freely exerts a powerful influence, thus bringing about an appreciation and greater acceptance of the presence of the United States in other areas. Hegemony is the term used to describe this ready assimilation of the ruling ideology and culture by those who are being dominated. It implies consent, not force.

In opposition to hegemony stands resistance. To resist the foreigner, a set of beliefs and forms of behavior put distance between the colonizer and the colonized. Resistance may be cultural, military, economic, or psychological. It may be overt (as in revolts), or covert (as in conscious foot-dragging), or it simply may not exist. Most analyses cover the overt forms of rebellion, with the more subtle forms largely unnoticed or ignored. In this book I look at the tensions between hegemony and resistance as they are manifested in the way the sport of baseball is organized, played, and enjoyed.

Curiously, Dominicans seem to use the very forms and symbols of their cultural domination to promote resistance. The reasons why resistance takes this particular route are not hard to see. Because baseball is the only area in which Dominicans come up against Americans and demonstrate superiority, it fosters national pride and keeps foreign influence at bay. But the resistance is incomplete. At an organizational level American baseball interests have gained power and are now unwittingly dismantling Dominican baseball. Therefore, just when the Dominicans are in a position to resist the influence of foreigners, the core of their resistance is slipping away into the hands of the foreigners themselves.

The organization of this book is straightforward. It is both a structural and a cultural assessment of sport in society. The first chapter contains an overview of the political and economic history of the Dominican Republic from colonial times to 1950, including the introduction and development of baseball. In chapter 2 I explore the way the game is structured, as well as how its present organization has evolved since the 1950s during three discrete periods. A series of crises in Dominican baseball is described and analyzed in chapter 3. Chapter 4 focuses on the Dominican baseball academy, which is both an agent of development and a symptom of underdevelopment. As I follow the rookies from their entrance into the academy through their passage to the United States, I examine the cultural and professional problems they must face. I focus especially on one of the Dominicans' most influential baseball figures: Ralph Avila, whom many view as the most well-rounded baseball man in the Caribbean.

In chapters 2, 3, and 4 I look at the hegemonic aspects of the game as it is currently organized and played in the Dominican Republic. Chapter 5 deals with the main obstacle to hegemony: the cultural resistance of the fans, the news media, and the players themselves. I argue that this resistance is critical to the efforts of the Dominicans to retain their hold on the game.

The subject of chapter 6 is Quisqueya Stadium, the largest and most important baseball facility in the Dominican Republic and the hub of baseball in the country. This chapter is an impressionistic ethnographic sketch; it situates the reader in the subculture of baseball in the capital city of Santo Domingo, to capture the flavor of the game and of Dominican culture. In looking at the various elements that make up the stadium culture, we see that they also serve who only stand and cheer: the spectators make their own vital contribution to the pride of their culture and country in the game. In chapter 7 I pull together the conclusions of the book and place them within the context of other studies of hegemony and resistance.

The Social Context of Sport in Society

The place of sport in society is problematic, for it is only during the last fifteen years that a more serious study of sport has begun. Since that time sport studies in the social sciences have encountered resistance in the same measure as other studies of popular culture have. Rather than develop a siege mentality, sports scholars have compiled an impressive record of accomplishment in situating sport as an active societal agent.

For better or worse, sport in America draws an enormous amount of cultural attention, and its share of the economic pie is significant: sport and related events and products are a multibillion dollar industry. In other countries the relation of sport to society is fiscally less impressive, but politically and culturally more involved.

Many outside the field of sports sociology view sport as a mirror of society. They see sport as an intrinsically conservative institution that both reflects and bolsters societal values and norms. Thus the extreme competitiveness of athletic events in the United States is thought to be consistent with the emphasis on individual advancement and winning that prevails in American society, just as the lack of competitiveness in Navajo Indian games is thought to be consistent with the cooperative nature of Navajo society. The idea that sport is a prop for the societal status quo, that sport and society enjoy a functional relationship and send signals to each other, is not so much erroneous as it is incomplete and outdated. In this book I take a different view, one now shared by most sports sociologists: that the function of sport is complex, that sport simultaneously reflects and obscures social and cultural phenomena. This view is consistent with what is known in the social sciences as the conflict perspective, and in the field of sports sociology it is supplanting the notion that the conflicts inherent in the relations between sport and society can be ignored or explained away.

The complex relations between sport and society are apparent in the controversy surrounding the illicit use by athletes of anabolic steroids.

The use of steroids in the National Football League and in the Olympic
Games of 1988 created a scandal, but perhaps most informative is the
use of steroids by bodybuilders, for the bodybuilding establishment has
institutionalized the use of these drugs while denying that it has done
so. The entrepreneurs and promoters who are responsible for projecting
the sport's image fill the magazines and television screens with pictures
of wholesome and healthy bodies. In this way they consciously try to
mirror mainstream values, to make bodybuilding symbolize the socially
accepted path to success and the virtues of hard work, discipline, and
sacrifice. But I have found that the wholesome, mainstream image of
bodybuilding is contrary to its reality.[2] The image serves to conceal the
corruption of values—widespread abuse of steroids, politicking, cheating, opportunism—and even when corruption is detected it is sometimes justified by appeals to the most cherished value of all: the pursuit
of victory. Thus oversubscribing to values justifies violating them. The
abuse of steroids by professional football players is explained in this way:
taking steroids is seen as the price one has to pay to succeed in the National Football League.[3]

Perhaps nowhere does sport obfuscate social realities as much as in
the racial area. Sport is one of few institutions in American society in
which blacks are overrepresented, particularly in the three most popular
sports: football (54 percent of the players are black), basketball (76 percent are black), and baseball (20 percent are black). If ever an institution
was successfully integrated, sport would appear to be it. Yet behind
these impressive statistics lies a discriminatory phenomenon called
"stacking";[4] its discovery by sports sociologists is perhaps their most important contribution. Stacking consists of assigning to whites the positions on a team that have organizational responsibilities, and relegating
to blacks those that require biological gifts such as speed and quickness,
as well as those that depend on the central positions occupied by whites.
Basketball has only recently overcome this tendency, and in other sports
stacking and racism are still pervasive. By creating the impression that
integration is more widespread than it really is, stacking therefore obscures a fundamental social reality. In some ways baseball plays a similarly deceptive role in the Dominican Republic.

Overview and Origins

A Brief History of
the Dominican Republic
and Béisbol

● ● ● ● ● ● ● ● ●

The history of Caribbean baseball is so closely tied to that of sugar cane that the sport might well be called sugarball. In most areas of Cuba, Puerto Rico, and the Dominican Republic, baseball grew up in the sugar refineries (ingenios).

Despite its underdeveloped condition the Dominican Republic has always had the resources to achieve economic autonomy,[1] and its failure to have done so can be traced to its colonial heritage. A Caribbean country with a population of almost seven million and an area of about eighteen thousand square miles (roughly the size of New Hampshire and Vermont combined), the Dominican Republic is a topographically varied place. Half the country is made up of mountainous terrain. There are four impressive mountain ranges (see map), of which the largest, the Cordillera Central, accounts for a third of the country's land mass. From these mountains come a variety of ores. The first Spanish settlers looked for gold and found it; later the list of sought-after metals came to include silver, copper, nickel, bauxite, and eventually ferronickel.[2]

The lowlands and valleys formed by the mountains are equally impressive, especially in the Cibao, a region roughly in the north central part of the country that covers some two thousand square miles and is known as the breadbasket of the Dominican Republic. The richest alluvial soils and farmlands in the Cibao are found east of Santiago de los

The Dominican Republic

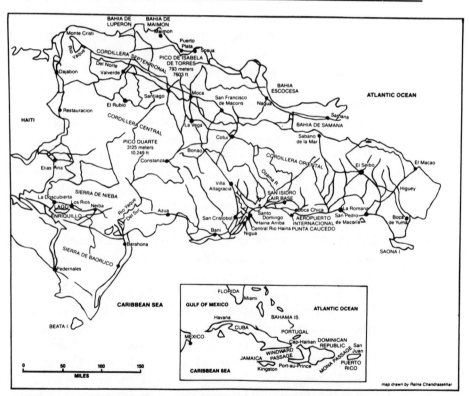

Reprinted from Michael J. Kryzanek and Howard J. Wiarda, *The Politics of External Influence in the Dominican Republic* (Praeger Publishers, N.Y., an imprint of Greenwood Publishing Group, 1988), p. 4.
© 1988 Praeger Publishers. Reprinted with permission of Greenwood Publishing Group.

Caballeros, where coffee, tobacco, cacao, and other crops are easily grown. To the west of the city one finds excellent pasture land for cattle.

The country is blessed with a maritime climate (temperatures average seventy-five degrees year-round), moderate rainfall in most places (modified by higher elevations), and trade winds, giving it a variety of conditions suitable for diversified agriculture.[3] On the large eastern coastal plain of more than a thousand square miles, where the land is ideal for sugar cane, the massive plantations and refineries are situated around La Romana and San Pedro de Macorís. The seas around the Dominican Republic offer an abundance of marine life, which is harvested for local use as well as for export. Several industries other than agriculture and fishing hold promise, including mining, tourism, and the raising of cattle.

Labor is also abundant. Despite Ronald Reagan's Caribbean Basin Initiative, which was aimed at giving American manufacturers access to cheap Caribbean labor, around 30 percent of the Dominican labor force remains unemployed, and around 50 percent is underemployed. The proportion of Dominicans who live in poverty has been estimated variously as being from 25 percent to 80 percent of the total population.[4] In any event it is clear that the resource base of the Dominican Republic and a plethora of externally induced programs have done little to ease the economic burdens of the country's citizens.

The poor have always been not only numerous but racially distinct: poverty is most widespread among mulattos (75 percent of the total population) and blacks (10 percent). The richest Dominicans are whites (15 percent), many of whom come from families dating back to the original Spanish landowning class of the sixteenth century. Something approximating an aristocracy emerged around Santiago in the nineteenth century, when highly skilled Cuban immigrants intermarried with Dominican landholders. On the southern coast Santo Domingo also had become a city of wealthy landowners: they earned their fortunes in sugar and later in commerce.

The middle class emerged during the regime of the dictator Rafael Trujillo and remains small and vulnerable. Trujillo intimidated the traditional aristocracy and favored instead the urban class, especially in the capital. A middle class of civil servants and managers took shape as he built the governmental sector and advanced the financial interests of Santo Domingo (which he renamed Ciudad Trujillo), and this group became more easily identifiable as the city drew increasing numbers of poor, displaced farmers. In general the middle class aped the tastes and aesthetics of the more affluent, though none of its members could afford more than cheap imitations of the latest European and American fashions. As in other countries this class sought upward mobility, but its small numbers and precarious economic and political position curbed its ability to gain it.

The religious and cultural life of the Dominican Republic is dominated by Roman Catholicism, and many religious festivals are celebrated: Holy Week, Altagracia, the Crowning of Our Lady of Mercedes. Until 1967 there were twenty-two legal holidays, many lasting more than one day (Christmas typically goes on for twelve), which underscores the Caribbean penchant for festivities. The most popular leisure activities include merengue (the national music and dance form), cock fighting, Carnival, and, perhaps most important, the sport of baseball. "It has only half jokingly been observed that there had never been a revolution during the baseball season."[5] Like other national and cultural forms, baseball helps to unite disparate social groups and regions of the country. But throughout the history of the Dominican Republic it has done more than simply promote consensus.

A Historical Overview of the Dominican Republic

The people of the Dominican Republic are proud that their country has been the site of many firsts. Incongruously and sadly, it has also been in many ways last or among the last. It was in the colony of Santo Domingo that the first city in the hemisphere was founded (1496), as well as the first cathedral (1523) and the first university (1538); and it is the Dominican Republic that has the lowest income per capita in the hemisphere ($1,222), one of the lowest literacy rates (68 percent), and one of the lowest rates of life expectancy (about 63 years). How a land so rich in resources and people, so endowed at the outset, could have failed to live up to its potential is the story not only of the Dominican Republic but of the colonial world as a whole.

The cultural accomplishments of the colony of Santo Domingo were short-lived although nevertheless quite real. Having gained preeminence virtually upon its founding, Santo Domingo within fifty years had lost its political supremacy.[6] The native population, once flourishing, was brutally treated and became extinct. The economic primacy of Santo Domingo was lost as more abundant sources of gold were discovered in Mexico and Peru. In 1564 an earthquake destroyed Santiago. (The history of the island Columbus called Hispaniola is one of repeated calamities, both man-made and natural. The city of Santo Domingo was ravaged by a hurricane in 1930 and by another in the 1970s.) From 1586 a chronic plague of pirates further weakened the economy of the colony.

By far the biggest external problem facing the Spanish colony was the irrepressible presence of the French on the western third of the island. In short order the French wrested control over the area and by 1697 formally declared it a French colony. This occurred just as Spain and France signed the Treaty of Ryswick, which ended a twelve-year war between them. From that time the Spanish side of the island was known as Santo Domingo, the French side as San Domingue. San Domingue became the richest colony in the Caribbean and possibly the New World, while Santo Domingo wallowed in neglect and was steadily wracked by internal squabbling.

The key to understanding the disparity in colonial fortunes lies in the rise of the sugar industry. Sugar cane was introduced from the Canary Islands in 1505.[7] Once on the island of Hispaniola it was enthusiastically taken on by the Jerónimo priests, who were responsible for the initial growth of the sugar industry.[8] The primary interest of the colonists at the time was not sugar, however, but gold. Spain maintained an overly restrictive control of its colonies and insisted on having returned to it all of their resources. So it was that the sugar, tobacco, and cacao that seemed to thrive in Santo Domingo ended up in Spanish ports, thus retarding the development of the colony.[9] The tight control of the crown stands in contrast to the relationship the the French crown had to its colony of San Domingue a few centuries later. There the colonists were not hampered in their search for external markets for trade, and its sugar industry grew rapidly. The massive importation of slaves was a direct result of this phenomenal growth.

Santo Domingo's sugar industry languished, handcuffed by the Spanish crown in its search for markets. As late as 1783 Santo Domingo had only nine ingenios, eleven *trapiches* (smaller sugar mills) in the sugar-producing lands of the east, and a mere six hundred slaves working in the industry. By comparison, San Domingue in 1790 had some 723 ingenios and at least 500,000 slaves.[10]

Relations between San Domingue (later Haiti) and Santo Domingo (later the Dominican Republic) had been steadily acrimonious, punctuated by periods of tolerance. Seeking the rights that French citizens had won in the French Revolution, the free mulattos of San Domingue agitated stridently in 1791. The slaves in the colony, in league with the free mulattos, then took up arms on their own behalf. The large number of slaves, so advantageous to the slave owners, had become the undoing of the colony. In 1804 San Domingue became Haiti, the first black republic. Slavery was abolished and sugar production plummeted. The rapid rise to economic prominence of the French colony had made the Spanish uneasy, but it was not until the slave revolt and subsequent revolution by the blacks of San Domingue that the Spanish became truly alarmed.

Meanwhile there had been a revival of the sugar industry in Santo Domingo during the latter part of the eighteenth century, which also triggered a demand for slaves.[11] When San Domingue pushed for the abolition of slavery, the substantially increased ranks of slaves in Santo Domingo voiced their support. There followed a series of invasions of Santo Domingo by San Domingue beginning in 1801, and these continued after Haiti won independence; the longest invasion lasted from 1822 to 1844. Much of the animosity that Dominicans feel toward Haitians dates to these invasions. Although the Haitians were the objects of hatred, it was during their occupation of Santo Domingo that a modern constitution was forged and Dominican slavery was ended.

Until the end of the nineteenth century Santo Domingo had a traditional two-class society, consisting of landed gentry and peasants, along with feudalistic property relations. Columbus and his cohorts had instituted a system of land ownership called *repartimiento*, under which settlers were granted large tracts of land along with the labor of the Native Americans on it (an arrangement that amounted to slavery). This established the traditional Latin American colonial system of the latifundia, which in 1503 the Spanish crown replaced with a similar one that enabled the landed class to stay in place.[12] There were also communal lands, which allowed peasants to have joint access to smaller tracts of land, but these were used to supplement a meager subsistence rather than as a real alternative to the larger plantations that had evolved by the late nineteenth century.

When not wracked by external conflicts and natural disasters, the Dominican Republic was tormented by internal factionalism. Regional politics have always had a profound impact on the internal affairs of Caribbean nations.[13] The three founding fathers of the Dominican Republic who rid their people of the Haitians in 1844 quickly fell upon each other. So chaotic and petty were the contending factions that their squabbling led to a brief reannexation of the republic by Spain in 1861. By 1865 the Spanish were suffering heavy losses from yellow fever and were no longer able to make plain their utility to the Dominicans. As a result the Spanish were again expelled and the republic declared sovereign. There followed renewed internecine struggles as rival *caudillos* (local strongmen and their retainers) vied with each other for control over a steadily weakening economy.

In the wake of the Cuban Civil War of 1868, which was fought over slavery, a wave of Cubans emigrated to the Dominican Republic. These new arrivals were members of the slave-owning, sugar-planting class on their island, and they were responsible for mechanizing the backward Dominican sugar industry.[14] In Europe the war between Germany and France in 1870 cut European sources of sugar, creating an external demand that Dominicans saw as a potential windfall. The Dominican government quickly tried to stimulate capital investments in the sugar industry to meet this unprecedented demand.[15] This meant that the refineries came under foreign control (mostly Cuban, Italian, and American). Around this time the investments and presence of the United States in the Dominican Republic began in earnest.

Over the next thirty years (1870–1900) the sugar industry rode a roller coaster as world market prices fluctuated widely. This helped shake out many of the smaller investors in the Dominican Republic, including the Cubans, leaving the Americans as the most powerful foreign influence in the country. Americans began to concentrate their holdings in everything having to do with the production and marketing of sugar cane, for example railroads and port facilities.[16] By 1900 the San Domingo Improvement Company, owned by the United States, was so diversified and the Dominican government was so indebted to it that the company took over the administration of the national customs revenues as security for its loans to the government. As its debts grew the Dominican government gave over increasing amounts of its revenues and administrative control to American companies, and this helped foster the growth of the sugar industry. The government's burgeoning debt led it to exempt American companies from taxes, and to make up for the loss of revenues the Dominican government taxed its own farmers and others to the hilt. As a result many of the smaller farmers were displaced, and their land was quickly bought up by American companies.[17] Internal strife resulted from this proletarianization of the peasants as well as from the economic ineptitude of the Dominican government. It became so widespread by 1916 that the U.S. Marines invaded the country on the pretext of securing the collection of customs revenues due the American government. The Marines also discouraged any attempt by Germany to gain a toehold on Hispaniola and threaten access to the Panama Canal.[18]

The Marine invasion of the Dominican Republic lasted eight long years (Haiti too was invaded, for fifteen years between 1916 and 1934), and to this day remains a source of resentment among many Dominican nationalists. It brought about numerous changes, including the creation of a national constabulary. Among the first recruits to the constabulary was the man who later became the very symbol of the Latin American dictator: Rafael Leónidas Trujillo Molina. As he moved up through the ranks of the National Police, Trujillo cleverly and brutally gained control of the country's political leadership and wealth. He successfully ruled the country from 1930 to 1961,[19] during which time he amassed a family fortune of a billion to one and a half billion dollars, including 75 percent of the country's sugar refineries.[20] To accomplish

this Trujillo forged a policy of forcing out the traditionally wealthy segments of Dominican society. He variously used and slaughtered thousands of Haitian workers in his country, and heightened nationalism when it strengthened his political hold.[21] Among the changes he wrought on the economic front was the fashioning of an economy dependent on a single crop, sugar. He also embarked on a series of the most ambitious building projects his country had ever known, and made the capital into a more modern city. The tyranny of his rule so outweighed his accomplishments, however, that by the 1950s he and his country grew politically and economically isolated. In May 1961 a small group of high-ranking officers (aided by the CIA) assassinated Trujillo as he was en route to a meeting with his mistress.[22]

Trujillo's demise left quite a void. A number of political figures mounted candidacies for the presidency, not the least of whom was Trujillo's son (he failed in his attempt to seize power). In 1962 hopes rose for increased economic redistribution and freedom of expression.

Joaquín Balaguer, an underling of Trujillo, attempted to capture the presidency by liberalizing the political climate and promising land distribution. Opposing him in the election of 1963 was a mildly left-of-center candidate, Juan Bosch, of the Dominican Revolutionary party (PRD). To the surprise of many, Bosch won. He sincerely hoped to guide the ship of state in an uneasy and suspicious sea. Bosch's greater tolerance for leftist elements in the country, however, enraged his right-leaning constituency. Fearing a takeover in the Dominican Republic similar to that of Castro in Cuba, Col. Elías Wessín y Wessín in a coup ousted Bosch in September 1963 after only seven months in office. Instability followed. In the spring of 1965 elements loyal to Bosch took to the streets to show their anger against the right wing.[23] The United States played a much more open role in this conflict than it did elsewhere. It not only agitated to oust Bosch but sent Marines into the country to make sure Bosch's supporters would not succeed in their efforts to regain power. After a two-year occupation, which not surprisingly spawned a good deal of anti-Americanism, the United States got the contending factions to agree to a new round of elections in 1966.

Hopes for a new era of prosperity were fueled again, only to be frustrated by a series of shallow presidencies highly dependent on the United States. From 1966 to 1978 Balaguer was in office. The first half of his term saw rapid growth caused by high prices for sugar. These were the result of Castro's revolution (which led the United States to turn away from Cuban sugar) and an influx of foreign loans. Large landowners expanded production in sugar and even more small farmers became displaced, swelling the population of Santo Domingo to 1.3 million (its current level).[24] By the mid-1970s high fuel prices began to threaten the gains made from sugar exports, and Balaguer's substantial following dropped. In 1978 Antonio Guzmán became president. A member of Bosch's old party the PRD, he brought back a tolerance for labor organizing but showed the same inability to deal with the Dominican Republic's weakening economic situation. The cost of oil imports had come to offset income from sugar, and all indications were that the world price of sugar was falling.[25] The policy of open-ended borrowing from the West that had so characterized the country's leaders before Guzmán was continued by him. Developing nations that pursue such an economic policy are eventually forced to seek aid from agencies such as the International Monetary Fund (IMF) in Washington, which generally grants loans on the condition that their recipients rein in spending. To the Dominican Republic this meant an austerity program, skyrocketing prices, and devaluation of the peso. Guzmán's successor, Jorge Blanco, continued these policies, as does the present administration of Balaguer.

These economic woes stemmed in large part from the Dominican Republic's overreliance on sugar production. Demand for sugar has fallen steadily since 1980, threatening to undo attempts by the country's leaders to alter their economic course. By 1984 sugar prices had fallen to four cents a pound, one-quarter of the cost of production.[26] At that point the island's largest investor, Gulf & Western, sold its massive La Romana sugar mill. To help buoy the flagging Dominican economy the United States began buying Dominican sugar at triple the world price; but this tactic also failed as demand for sugar in the United States declined. It seemed that if the Dominican Republic were to survive in the modern world it would have to wean itself from its historic overdependence on sugar. It is now attempting to do just this by promoting new industries, namely mining and tourism. Sugar now generates less revenue than these two industries, though it still generates a great deal. These economic attempts notwithstanding, life in the Dominican Republic has become more difficult for the average citizen as poverty, unemployment and underemployment, and inadequate health care have remained at least as severe as before. Basic services such as electricity and public transit have deteriorated in the past few years, to the point where Bosch's latest bid for the presidency, in 1990, was his strongest ever.[27]

The Dominican Republic is in many ways a classic case of underdevelopment, historically filled with internal struggle, corrupt, power-hungry leaders, and hardships for the vast majority of citizens. One sees everywhere the imprint of colonial powers (first Spain, now the United

States). Some aspects of the colonial legacy are unquestionably oppressive, such as the exploitative system built around the production of
sugar.

In other areas foreign domination seems more benign, even enjoy-
able; baseball appears to fall into this category. But baseball is inextrica-
bly bound up with the production of sugar. Its history is a microcosm of
Dominican-American relations.

Throughout the history of the Dominican Republic, factionalism
and turmoil have been interrupted only by periods of artificial stability
occasioned by autocratic rule. This was certainly the case in the last decade of the nineteenth century, when after seventeen years of dictatorial
rule by Gen. Ulises Heureaux the foreign debt of the country had
swollen to $32 million.[28] After his assassination in 1899 another period
of political instability ensued, as rival factions vied for control of an already sick economy. Dominican failings ultimately led to the direct intervention of the United States in the country shortly after the turn of
the century. It was within this ungainly context that Dominican baseball was born or, rather, dropped at the doorstep.

Slave revolts in Cuba in 1868 so threatened the members of the
planter class that thousands were forced to emigrate to the Dominican
Republic.[29] In his study of the political and economic history of sugar
cane in the region, Roger Plant points out that the Cubans brought with
them technology, capital, and an entrepreneurial drive for which they
are known throughout the Caribbean.[30] Cuban owners began to mecha-
nize their sugar mills in 1876; fifteen years later mechanized mills were
common in the eastern part of the country. Until then American companies had made only marginal investments in the area, but when they
saw the improvements made by the Cubans they quickly leapfrogged
over their less capitalized, less powerful Cuban competitors and from
them wrested control of the sugar trade. In a related development the
Westendorp Corporation, a firm based in Amsterdam that was the Dominican Republic's largest creditor in 1892, went bankrupt in that year
and had its Dominican interests bought by American investors.[31]

In the beginning of the twentieth century the political role of baseball
was best captured in the musings of the sport's pioneer entrepreneur
A. G. Spaulding, who believed baseball should "follow the flag."[32] In
this capacity baseball was introduced into Japan and the Caribbean in
the final decade of the nineteenth century, as testament to American
political and cultural superiority. There have been several distinct phases
in the history of Dominican baseball, each with a slightly different character, but all contributing to the current state of the game.

Disorganized Roots: 1891 to 1920

A unique combination of Americans and Cubans was responsible for
the presence of baseball in the Dominican Republic. The game was first
brought to the Dominican Republic in the final months of 1891 by the
Aloma brothers, two Cubans who worked there.[33] Baseball had been
played in Cuba since American troops stationed there introduced it in
the 1860s. It was easy for the Dominicans to adopt the game in part
because they were culturally close to the Cubans, and in part because
baseball was the game invented and played by the Americans, the symbols of power who were increasingly present. During the next few years
the Cubans taught the game to their neighbors; they even formed two
teams—the Cervecería (brewery) and the Cauto (named after a river in
Cuba)—which would play each other throughout Santo Domingo.

The first professional Dominican team was Licey, organized sometime in 1907 and named after an Indian word for a small but turbulent
river in the country. The notable Dominican baseball historian Cúqui
Córdova says that Licey was formed by a group of sportsmen in Santo
Domingo in response to the formation of another team, the amateur
Nuevo Club.[34] Vicioso and Alvarez, however, point out that Nuevo Club
was not begun until four years after Licey.[35] (Discrepancies such as this
are frequent among baseball chroniclers in the Dominican Republic.)

In its early days baseball was organized along lines that were nothing
like those of the present, as teams were constantly formed and re-formed
at both the amateur and semiprofessional levels and had to work to establish a wide following throughout the country. Often teams would
simply square off in a tournament, with the number of games varying
from one tournament to the next. By 1911 there were at least three formal teams, for in that year a team from San Pedro de Macorís was
formed; it played against Licey and Nuevo Club in 1912 in the country's
first formal series;[36] Nuevo Club won two out of three games from Licey
to win this local "championship."[37] Nuevo Club disbanded in 1916; a
new club, San Carlos, was in operation from 1917 to 1920.

Amateur baseball thrived in and around the major cities of Santo Domingo, San Pedro de Macorís, and Santiago. Teams such as Capital,
Amor al Progreso, Santo Domingo, and Gimnasio Escolar were some
of the more frequently mentioned. These teams seem to have been
closer to a professional level than amateur teams are now. For instance,
the Dominican baseball historians Vicioso and Alvarez point out that
members of the amateur teams Los Muchachos and Delco Light were
among those chosen in 1921 to make up the professional team Escogido
(the name means "the chosen" in Spanish), along with members from
the recently defunct professional team San Carlos.[38]

This era also saw the beginning of intra-Caribbean competition. In

1920 Puerto Rican and Cuban professional teams visited the Dominican Republic for a series of exhibition games. In playing teams from
the other Caribbean islands the Dominican Republic found a way
of demonstrating excellence. Introduced to the game after Cuba and
Puerto Rico, the Dominican Republic initially looked to them both for
guidance and as a way of measuring its own progress. Each time the
highly touted teams from Cuba came to the country for an exhibition
series, it was as if the state of the game were being examined by the
entire Caribbean.

Whether amateur or professional, these early contests were avidly followed and hard fought. This is made clear in biographical sketches of
such players as the Nuevo Club's battery mates Paco Siragusa and Enri-
que Hernández ("El Indio Bravo"), both of whom were standouts in the
series with Licey in 1912.[39] But this contest was merely a prelude to the
"national" championship series between the representatives from the
capital, Nuevo Club, and the eastern challengers from San Pedro de
Macorís. The intense regional pride, emotionality, and fierce play for
which Dominicans are so well known were already present during this
series. In the first game Nuevo Club lost the home field advantage when
it was defeated by San Pedro's Estrellas Orientales. When Nuevo Club
lost the second game, a spirited contest in San Pedro de Macorís, it
proved too much to bear: the Nuevo Club alleged partiality on the part
of the umpires. So strenuous were their objections that the championship series was disrupted, and San Pedro was declared the winner of an
aborted tournament notable for the intense rivalry and passion displayed
by both players and fans.[40]

In 1914 the entire country took notice when Hernández pitched a
no-hit, no-run game against a team of Americans from the U.S. Navy
cruiser *Washington*.[41] This game later gained importance as a symbol of
Dominican resistance when the country was invaded by the U.S. Marines (see below).

1921 to 1937: Béisbol Rentada

Dominican baseball took on a more professional appearance in the 1920s
and 1930s. The game was being played more widely than ever before,
the players were increasingly of an impressive caliber, and politically
powerful and well-heeled patrons were beginning to acknowledge the
importance of the game. This move forward by Dominican baseball was
fitful, however. Periods of apparently genuine attempts at organized contests and increasingly systematized play would be interrupted by declines

and disorientation. The overall trend during this period was toward increased competence, but national events and economic conditions militated against sustained progress. Four straight national championship series were contested in the early 1920s, then interrupted by the Depression from 1929 to 1935.

The year 1921 was a watershed, not only because of the professionalization of the game that followed but because of the emergence of Escogido. Like Licey, Escogido was based in Santo Domingo, and the two teams soon developed a rivalry that became legendary; they are among the four professional teams that remain active (the others being Santiago and San Pedro de Macorís).

As with most events and people that are larger than life, there is a good deal of myth surrounding the emergence of Escogido. According to some popular accounts the team was formed because the petulant son of the country's dictator, Trujillo, could not earn a spot on Licey, and Trujillo conscripted players from all the other teams to fashion a team and give his son an opportunity to play. But Trujillo did not become the Dominican leader until 1930, nine years after Escogido came into existence, and his ties to baseball were minimal and indirect; he used baseball primarily to serve his own political ends. According to baseball historians in the Dominican Republic, it was Trujillo's brother who was a consummate fan and mentor.[42] "Trujillo, he only liked horses, not ballgames. But, he knew the people liked baseball. He was smart. He thought, 'I killed many people. I need to entertain people, to take their minds off of it. I'll do what I can to help push Dominican baseball.' He only went to one ballgame because the day before his brother hit an American player, and he was angry about it. He went so things would be quiet."[43] Vicioso and Alvarez find no baseball tie whatsoever between Escogido and Trujillo;[44] they assert that Escogido came into being when players from other teams were chosen to play a touring team of Cuban all-stars.

What Dominican sports historians call the eternal rivalry between the two teams from Santo Domingo was characterized by pomp, passion, unexpected turns and twists, and considerable mythology. The new team Escogido was an upstart and a rival to the hallowed Licey Tigers. The Tigers were the nation's oldest and most successful team, with a broad following in all social strata that was especially deep among the disenfranchised. Not only did the teams compete for the affections of the same fans, but their colors were the same as those of rival political parties (blue for Licey, red for Escogido).

In 1921 Licey and Escogido played two series: in the first each team won two games, in the second Licey won four and Escogido one. In the

second year of their rivalry the teams squared off for a nineteen-game
series between 9 April and 10 September 1922. Already contests between the two teams had the look of a widely followed national rite, and fans wondered whether the upstarts from Escogido had the wherewithal to defeat Licey.

The game played on 14 May had all the drama and pathos that can be expected of any game, and became emblematic of the rivalry between the blue and the red.[45] It came to be known as the "queen's championship," because the owner of Licey, convinced of his team's superiority, arranged to have a national beauty queen offer a toast at the game. This was to have the effect of simultaneously impressing and unnerving the opposition:

> A young woman, considered the most beautiful in the Republic, the Señorita Esperanza Pereyra, won the title of "Queen" in her native town of La Vega and was also crowned "Queen of queens" when she surpassed the other grand Dominican beauties. Esperanza was also proclaimed "Queen of Licey" and invited to be present at the game on the 14th. Don Geo Pou, president of the Blues [Licey], personally went to La Vega and drove the beauty queen to the capital in his car. Their arrival in Santo Domingo was a social event. The queen was to assist in the game, but couldn't make her entrance earlier. The managers of Licey were afraid of losing [the game], and only when they had a three-run lead in the eighth inning did the sovereign arrive to make the championship toast.[46]

By the end of the eighth inning Licey still clung to a two-run lead. It all but had the game won when a substitute outfielder for Licey, Loco Lamberto, misplayed a ball hit by Mateo de la Rosa of Escogido with the bases loaded. Three runs scored, Licey lost 6 to 5, Lamberto was made a goat for all time, and de la Rosa became known as "the batter that made the Queen cry." The beauty queen Esperanza saw her image soiled in fashionable Santo Domingo before thousands of grieving Licey fans, and she began to sob uncontrollably. She had no idea that she would become part of a legend much greater than that created by her reign as the most beautiful woman in the Dominican Republic.

Legends were born in a variety of ways. Fellito Guerra, for instance, was hailed as an athlete for what he did and as a patriot for what he refused to do. An outstanding pitcher, Guerra was well known for his duels with the highly respected Cuban team, which first visited the Dominican Republic in 1920 (he pitched a four-hitter), and then with the Puerto Ricans and North Americans. Stories of his exploits were told in towns all over the country. When as a result of his accomplishments he was asked to play in the United States (the highest compliment a player could receive), everyone in the Dominican Republic was pleased for him. But he refused, citing as a reason his opposition to the occupation of his country by the U.S. Marines. Crowds of Dominicans similarly outraged with the occupation hailed him wherever he went, and Guerra was adulated as a virtual deity.[47]

Having learned baseball later than the Cubans, Puerto Ricans, and Panamanians, the Dominicans were at first looked on in other Latin American countries as students of the game, and no foreign teams visited them until 1920. From then on, however, touring teams regularly made stops in the Dominican Republic, where they found a sophisticated level of play and abundant talent. The Dominican press was eager to make a superstar of any Dominican who prevailed over these visitors. Abejita Ruiz, a left-handed pitcher touted as having the best curve ball of his day, was the sort of player the powerful Cuban and Venezuelan teams had to face. On 24 September 1933 he pitched against the highly regarded Puerto Rican team Ponce, and won, 7 to 2. Six weeks later he beat the Cuban Stars, 6 to 5. In the following February he faced what many considered the finest Latin American team of all time, the Venezuelan team of Concordia. Although Concordia was loaded with such stars as Tetelo Varga and Luis Aparicio (father of the American Leaguer of the 1960s), and *importados* like Josh Gibson of the Negro Leagues, Ruiz beat Concordia 6 to 2 with a dazzling array of curves set up with a precise fastball.[48]

From 1920 Dominican stars were increasingly found on the rosters of teams in Puerto Rico, Cuba, and Venezuela. Often the owners of foreign teams were so taken with the performance of their Dominican opponents that they offered them the chance to play for their own clubs. One example is Diógenes Lara, who while touring Puerto Rico with the team Dominican Stars in 1922 so impressed the owners of the Puerto Rican team Humacao that they signed him for the 1923 season. He played professionally in Venezuela in 1927 between long stays with Escogido.[49] At the same time foreign players were becoming increasingly common in Dominican baseball: by the mid-1930s Cubans and Negro Leaguers were playing for Dominican teams.[50]

The term *béisbol rentada* is used to refer to the brand of organized or semiorganized professional baseball played in this period. Large sums of money were needed to pay the rapidly escalating salaries of players, and although money was coming in through the gates it was not always enough.[51] As competition for players at home and abroad intensified, more cash was needed. Owners caught up in the quest for championship titles were at times pushed beyond their means. When this

happened they sought the support of powerful business and government interests, such as the Antún family in San Pedro de Macorís and the Trujillos in Santo Domingo.

The fierce competition to sign players and win championships was heightened considerably when stars from the Negro Leagues began to sign contracts in the Dominican Republic, but the sobering political and economic conditions in the country threatened to bring the bidding to a halt. The depression of the 1920s and 1930s interrupted the national championships between 1929 and 1935. During this time professional play continued, but only at the level of the individual series.[52]

By 1936, however, the competition for national championships was renewed by such rich owners as those of the Estrellas Orientales in San Pedro de Macorís, who spent lavishly to sign four of the best Cuban players of the time as well as Dominican luminaries such as the outfielder Tetelo Vargas and Mateo de la Rosa. To no one's surprise San Pedro won the championship that year, which was followed immediately by the most spectacular season in the history of Dominican baseball.

The 1937 Season

If ever there was a sports season in which the passions of owners, players, and fans alike were indulged to the fullest, it was the Dominican baseball season of 1937. Owners bought the best foreign talent available, cultures clashed, political intrigue was rampant, and the level of play was taken to unprecedented heights.

The impact of this season was felt far beyond the shores of the Dominican Republic. In discussing the effect of the Dominican excesses on the Negro Leagues, Donn Rogosin posits a political motive: "Facing one of the toughest fights in his political career [Trujillo] decided to enhance his reputation by winning the Dominican pennant."[53] Dominican sources more familiar with the times point out that there were more complicated and diverse factors at work, not the least of which was the championship blood lust that owners had aroused among themselves in the preceding year.[54]

Trujillo's notorious lack of interest in the game was more than outweighed by the passion for it shown by his brother, an insatiable fan and the primary economic force behind Licey. So uncontrollable were his emotions that he created something of a national embarrassment by striking an American player in public: "Trujillo's brother and sister sponsored Licey in those days. If [Licey] needed money, Trujillo's brother gave it to them. After Trujillo's brother got into a problem about an American playing there Trujillo didn't want his brother involved with the team anymore." [55]

In 1937 agents from various Dominican teams came to the United States to lure the great black ballplayers. Satchel Paige, by far the biggest prize on the Dominican shopping list, was signed for more than $1000 a month. Also on the list were Cool Papa Bell and Josh Gibson. The impact of these defections to the Dominican Republic was instantly felt in the Negro Leagues: "Since the best players were already in The Dominican Republic, the cause of the [Pittsburgh] Crawfords was hopeless, and the team dropped from the Negro League shortly thereafter." [56] Dominican sources corroborate these accounts. The following excerpt from an interview with the Dominican baseball historian Córdova gives a sense of how far the hunt for foreign talent and prestigious championships had gone:

> There was so much enthusiasm here in that year that [the owners] went to all the countries to bring ballplayers here: from Cuba, Puerto Rico, Venezuela, and the States. All the ballplayers were here playing for the three teams: Estrellas Orientales, Santiago, and Ciudad Trujillo. Ciudad Trujillo were the champs. They were called the Ciudad Trujillo Dragons. You see, Licey and Escogido were fighting and they finally agreed to mix the teams, calling it the Ciudad Trujillo Dragons. This lasted only for the 1937 season. By the end of the season only two Dominican players were playing: Tetelo Vargas and Horacio Martínez. All the rest were Cubans or Americans. And the Negro Leagues had to stop playing because all the good players were here. [57]

Reports of the wild thirty-six game series among the three teams verged on the epic. The games were hotly contested and rife with exploits off the field and on it (Rudolfo Fernández saving Ciudad Trujillo with a breathtaking pitching performance that earned him the nickname "watched by God"), as well as political intrigues and games forfeited because of unruly fans.

Rogosin describes the stories that made the rounds among black American players; among other things they included accounts of intimidation and threats by Trujillo's men. According to one of these stories a loss by American players prompted the police to fire their weapons into the air, shouting, "The President doesn't like to lose." In addition, the police reputedly jailed players to make sure they did not carouse all night long.[58] Dominican writers were rankled by the accounts of life in the Dominican Republic of black American players (particularly Paige), some of which were no doubt exaggerated: "Paige talked baloney. Many of the things he said weren't true. One of the things he said is that they were at a ballgame and there were snakes crawling around. I never saw a snake in the Dominican Republic. We have them only in the jungle, but we don't play ball in the jungle. And he also said everybody is armed. That's baloney."[59] "Satchel Paige was lying. We call it 'Línea de cala' [load line]. He talked about taking trains here in Santo Domingo. There were none. He talked about the president's men shouting and threatening them. They never did. Línea de cala."[60]

The championship won by the Ciudad Trujillo Dragons culminated a season that seemed simultaneously to fulfill and to exhaust professional baseball in the Dominican Republic. While the crowds in the capital danced in the streets and carried on as if during Carnival, the game slid into an abyss:"All those players like Paige, Perkins; they received more money to play here than in the U.S. It was crazy, but at the same time we had what we felt were the best teams in the world. We wound up killing professional baseball here. Although we continued to play amateur ball, we spent many years without professional ball after 1937. Even Licey and Escogido only played occasionally. The 1937 championship stopped baseball. All our money was gone. We were exhausted financially and in enthusiasm also."[61]

1938 to 1950: The Era of Decline

The crisis that beset organized national baseball after the frenzy and high costs of the formidable season of 1937 lasted for thirteen years.[62] Amateur play at the local level, however, continued; one could even argue that the period of professional decline helped it. That amateur baseball flourished in these hard times shows that the passions Dominicans have for their game are not mediated by money or international acclaim.

Licey and Escogido temporarily merged for the 1937 season and then resumed play against each other, though only as amateurs—in 1938 (for the Palatine Series, which lasted fifteen games), and again in 1940. By then new clubs of a fairly high caliber had been formed that seemed again to satisfy the public's desire for competition. In the course of haphazard but intense rivalry between clubs the best players were selected to represent the Dominican Republic in international events, the most prestigious of which was the Amateur World Series (Serie Amateo

Mundial), played by teams from all over Latin America. Other tournaments also were eagerly followed in the local press.

Despite the nationalist energies put forth in play against other countries, a localism characterized this period of decentralized amateur competition (known as the era of the *regionales*). All sorts of teams were formed by townships (La Vega), by cities (Santiago and San Pedro de Macorís), and by companies (the Presidente brewery and, perhaps most important, the refineries).

The best baseball was played by the same four teams as before. Teams like Licey and Escogido were no longer strictly professional but rather semiprofessional. Predictably, the better players sought actively to sign with them as well as with fully professional clubs in Puerto Rico, Cuba, and elsewhere. Hence in one of the legendary showdowns of the period, a game in 1942 between La Vega and Santiago in which the best players in the country were pitted against each other, Tetelo Vargas, arguably the best player of the day, was conspicuously absent: he was off playing professionally in Puerto Rico.[63] There was no problem when Vargas returned later that year to play in his homeland, his amateur status intact.

Even as amateur organizations the four teams continued to have the backing of powerful families, and as a result they attracted the best players from outlying areas. Thus the backing of Trujillo's brother and other members of the elite from Ciudad Trujillo enabled Licey to recruit players from the armed forces baseball squads, which in turn recruited players from townships like La Vega; this allowed Licey to draw on a wide pool of talent.[64]

Throughout most of the history of Dominican baseball, organization has been sorely lacking. There was no consistent schedule, teams came and went, and there was little formal structure or governance of play. It was perhaps to disguise this as well as to reflect the war effort abroad that in the 1940s a series of meetings between two clubs was often given a grand-sounding title. In 1943, for example, a series between La Vega and Santiago was called "V for Victory."[65]

The 1940s saw culture and the press concentrated in Ciudad Trujillo (and to a lesser extent in Santiago), which gave contemporary descriptions of baseball a decided orientation toward the capital. This provincialism notwithstanding, the brand of baseball played in the sugar cane area around San Pedro de Macorís could not be surpassed. Córdova concedes, "Yes, the majority of good players came from sugar mills in San Pedro . . . Remember one thing, all those good players from sugar refineries are very poor. They are hungry. They put more enthusiasm into it."[66] One lifelong baseball promoter and organizer from the refineries put this in the context of the country's rigid class distinctions:

"[Journalists in the big cities] only recognized the ingenios when our players got to the big leagues. In spite of our people who become famous and rich players, Antún and others still say they are nothing. In our country they only recognize those who are professionals, powerful politicians, owners. They don't recognize those who are small. The small person who is poor, we call 'el menos.' They have no importance."[67]

Cane Ball in the Refineries

In the cane fields baseball began as a diversion supplied by refinery managers for their men during the slack harvest period. But the familial, close-knit nature of the communities that grew around the refineries fostered an identification with the baseball players and teams, and this intensified the game. Angelina, Consuelo, La Paja, Quisqueya, and others developed a rivalry that was unmatched elsewhere.

One notable promoter of baseball in the 1940s was Austin Jacobo, who helped introduce the game at his refinery in Consuelo. He began living and working in New York in the early 1970s, and has continued to contribute goods and services to his home community. His descriptions of life and baseball in Consuelo show the intense love of the game felt by the refinery workers, which is more impressive in the light of the poverty and arduous labor they had to endure daily as they eked out a living:

> At that time things were very hard for us. Then we didn't have school except up to third grade. We were descendants of British Caribbean poor people.
>
> So to survive you cut cane. Then in the season when they didn't have cane, you hoed and weeded. But in Trujillo's time when he bought the estates he cut all that. He brought in germicides to kill the grass, so then life was really hard for us. The people just stayed there [and had no livelihood during the slack season]. We played ball. We suck[ed] cane and people would plant vegetables in the backyards. We survived and everything was honest.
>
> In Consuelo it was the American Sugar Company [before Trujillo bought the refinery]. And, as you know, Americans like baseball. We played too. We played "regionales." Each town [refinery] had a team. So, the estate of Consuelo used to provide one team with uniforms, gloves, and so on. But that couldn't fill the needs of the majority of the people because out there we only

had two choices: you either play baseball or you cut cane in the plantation.

Right down to 1942 [when] we got a Canadian priest. That was the first Catholic church we had. He saw that the people liked sports, and he started to get us together. . . . So we asked him if he could get us uniforms and equipment. He was named Father Joseph Ensley . . . the priest what I speak to you about . . . he taught us that we shouldn't be a slave. He taught us that we should be on our own. He said, "No, you do it by yourself. You must not be a beggar. What you will do is that during the season you start to save a quarter a week." And when the season finished he would go and buy a big bolt of cloth . . . So we start to save those quarters, and the next season, which is the dull season, he said to go make the uniforms. And the uniforms come out, and I tell you from that time on we start to play and go out to San Pedro de Macorís, Santa Fe, Angelina.

[The refinery] is where the players belong to. They don't belong to San Pedro de Macorís as you see published. They come from Consuelo, Santa Fe, Quisqueya, Las Pajas, Colón. [The organizers from San Pedro de Macorís] don't want to do anything for us, so we had to take care of our own baseball. We started to draft players from our ingenios. We had so many players in Consuelo that we didn't know what to do with them. We had to send them to other places so they would get a chance. When we started with the amateurs we got players like Chico Contón. He went to Cuba, Puerto Rico. He went all over but not to the majors. We had others too like Hilton Willey. He was the best player I ever saw including major leaguers.

We played a higher kind of baseball than they did in La Vega and those places because we had American influence in our brand of ball. We also had more support from Consuelo. Licey and Escogido was higher than us because they had political powers helping them, but we played with pride and felt second to no one. Look at who are the best these days—we, from the ingenios.[68]

On the style of play and ambience of the refineries:

These games [between refineries] were bigger than the World Series to us. When you go to one of these estates baseball was the only thing [diversion] you gonna see. There was no movies. So, everybody got into that. They didn't want coffee at the house, everybody was on the field. So when you lose a game, everybody crying or something; fighting or something.

If you go to Angelina and they win, they fight you. And if they
lose, they fight. It was because they was so excited, you know?
And if the umpire calls a bad play, you can bet you're gonna
fight. But out of that comes the bravery of these players; and
Angelina gave us this player Pedro Gonzales, and he played with
the New York Yankees 1964–65.[69]

Here are the recollections of Chico Contón, a player for Consuelo in
the 1950s:

Oh, we had rivals. Santa Fe and Porvenir were rivals so close to
each other. Our rival was Angelina. But those son-of-a-guns,
they don't know how to lose [nicely]. Each time they come over
we'd wind up in a fight. Always! Angelenos coming over and we
have to prepare for a fight. The fans always were pushing, yelling
and all that. They'd yell, "Get some good ball players! You're
walking barefoot! You don't have enough to eat!" It would get
hot, but not that we would really harm each other. We would
fight with fists, not with bats. If anybody grabbed a bat, we didn't
allow that. We get you off the team. We had disciplined fights.
But if they get one or two bad calls when they came to Consuelo,
prepare yourself for when you go to Angelina.

We had a lotta players who don't like to go to Las Pajas or
Quisqueya. Boy, those son-of-a-guns! They had umps that would
double play a guy ten yards from the base. We would tell the kids
to hustle and win the morning game—we used to play two
games—because you knew you were not gonna win the afternoon game.[70]

National and International Play

Amateur competition at the national level existed, but international and
local competition were given greater emphasis. International competition seemed to satisfy some of the passion for seeing the game played
above the purely local level. It was the goal of the really fine players to
play against teams from other countries, perhaps signing with them after
the contests and getting one foot in professional baseball. In 1944 the
Dominicans fielded a team of their best to compete in an international
series called the "Antilles Pearl," a seven-game affair against Cuba.[71]
The Dominicans took particular pleasure in playing the Cubans, who
lorded over other countries for having been the first in the region to play
baseball (and lorded in particular over the Dominicans for having intro-

duced the game to them). Moreover the Cubans were generally seen as invincible, having lost only two tournaments before (1926, 1941).

This time the Dominicans marshaled a particularly strong team that included many of their greatest players of all time. In the first game the Dominicans showed their offensive potential as they erupted for eight runs and held the Cubans to five. Pepe Lucas and the youngest of the three Grillo brothers (Luis Baéz, known as Grillo "C") each collected three hits in the winning effort, while their infield mate, the second baseman Aquiles Martínez, got two. In typical fashion the Dominicans fielded superbly and committed no errors.

After losing the second game the Dominicans came back in the third to beat Cuba 5 to 1. Andrés Julio Baéz, the middle Grillo brother (known as Grillo "B"), allowed the Cubans only four hits and was the winning pitcher. The fourth game of the series was won 8 to 4 by the Dominican pitcher Loro Escalante, who had also won the first game. Once more the Dominicans overwhelmed the Cubans, who like most Latin American teams were unaccustomed to encountering teams that could manufacture many runs. The youngest Grillo again went four for five, as did Elucar Alvarez. The Dominicans slugged out eight runs for a third time in the very next game and held the opposition to three. In the sixth game the Cubans, already beaten in the series, tried desperately to salvage the final victories and save face. They won 5 to 2, behind the pitching of Yoyo O'Reilly. The final game pitted Grillo "B," pitching for the third time, against Mohím García and was the only close game of the series: the Dominicans prevailed, 4 to 3, winning the series convincingly by 5 games to 2.[72] This stunning victory served notice to the rest of Latin America that the Dominicans would be heard from again.

Although béisbol rentada was defunct in the Dominican Republic, Dominicans would often find lucrative prospects in neighboring countries.[73] Niño el Zurdo played in an Amateur World Series in Caracas and stayed there to play professionally. After winning a batting championship for the Dominicans in the Amateur World Series of 1948, Manuel Cáceres signed to play professionally in Puerto Rico the following year. In the years between 1938 and 1950 Tetelo Vargas, the Grillo brothers, Guigui Lucas, and many others balanced amateur or semiprofessional careers at home with professional seasons abroad. But this was the prerogative of the best players; for most a career was forged in the highly charged atmosphere of the regionales.

Clearly the regional nature of the game fostered strong local ties and gave a much more Dominican feel to the game, which flourished at the refineries around San Pedro de Macorís. This was in large part because baseball was not played professionally at the time: later the professional

game had the effect of destroying a healthy amateur system (see chapter
3). Professional baseball was still played abroad, however. The big four
(Licey, Escogido, San Pedro, Santiago), which were semiprofessional,
still had the best players, and international travel increased. Fewer importados were signed and more players went overseas to extend their careers and earn the salaries they had now come to expect.

International competition between Caribbean and Central American
countries matured during this era as well. In place of the flashy style of
professional ball that prevailed in 1937 there grew amateur competition
of a high level. This outstanding amateur play became the means for
the Dominicans to prove their mettle and overcome the late start they
had got in learning baseball. Confrontations with Puerto Rico and particularly with Cuba were much sought after as measures of how much
they had learned.

1951 to 1954: Béisbol Romántico

There is some confusion regarding the term *béisbol romántico*. Some
apply it only to Dominican baseball from 1951 to 1954,[74] others to all of
Dominican baseball before 1955.[75] Everyone agrees that the term de-
notes a brand of baseball stamped by Dominican organization (or lack
of it), values, passion, and play: "The way you play in our country is
you have to hustle: throw, run, hit. If you didn't, the team would release you. The fans would scream like hell. I remember the year before
Roger Maris hit 61 home runs. I was in center field and he was in right
field for the Estrellas Orientales. He played but he wasn't a hustler. He
played a month and they released him. He was a good ballplayer, but
not the way they like you to play in our country."[76]

The term *romántico* also bespeaks a unique bond between players
and fans that was born of the close-knit nature of communities in the
Dominican Republic. One professional of the 1950s described béisbol
romántico as follows:

> The people were so in love with the game. The way it was: when
> the ballgame is over, the fans wait for us. We go with them. We
> walk with them. And the people love ballplayers, and we them. It
> was like a family.
>
> I used to be standing on the corner talking with my friends
> after the ball game. Now, to see a ballplayer is mysterious. You
> can't see them. Then, the hotel was in the middle of the city. So,

when you get up in the morning people are waiting for you.
And you were talking to them. When Marichál came there, we
would go out and talk an hour and a half [with the fans] and
go home. It sure was different.[77]

Béisbol romántico was a distinctly Dominican cultural artifact, in
contrast with the game so dominated by the United States after 1955;
while no authors say so explicitly, the implication is that béisbol romántico is synonymous with Dominican cultural control.

Because Americans ignored Dominican baseball for the first half of
the twentieth century,[78] it was able to develop its distinctively Dominican
character. American baseball was of course followed in the Dominican
Republic, but at a distance—the racial segregation that marked it for so
long made it unapproachable.

In 1950 Dominican baseball took a giant step forward. On a visit to
Managua members of the Dominican national team met with a group
of sportsmen who accompanied them, and with other influential figures
such as the liquor magnate Julián Barcelo; together they resolved to
form in the following year a newly constituted professional Dominican
baseball league.[79] Under the guidance of a director general of sports, the
Commission of Professional Baseball (later to include the Dominican
League of Professional Baseball) gave the game a structure it had never
had before.

The Dominican professional league began with four teams (in three
cities) that played during the summer. The schedule was more systematic and symmetrical than it had been before: games were regularly
scheduled on weekends, there were two divisions, each with two teams,
and the season was divided into two rounds. During each round every
team played a schedule of twenty-seven games, some against teams in
the other division. The winners of the two divisions played against each
other in a national championship.[80]

This greater systematization both reflected and stimulated the desire
of many sports promoters and players to make professional baseball
teams from the Dominican Republic competitive with those of other
Latin American countries. To this end the Dominican government advanced as much as $200,000 to $300,000 to the teams so that they
might bid for the services of good ballplayers, the money to be repaid
from gate receipts during the season.[81]

The opportunities for Dominican players wrought by the integration
of American baseball were equally important. Although Dominicans
had played professional baseball in the United States since "Mero"
Urena played in the minor leagues in 1925,[82] Dominicans generally fell

under the ban prohibiting men of color from playing with whites in the

United States. This ban was aided by Trujillo's periodic discouragement of attempts by foreigners to sign Dominican players. There were Latino players in the United States, such as the Cuban Adolfo Luqué, but they were rare. But by the early 1950s Latinos with dark skin felt that a better future awaited them. Rudy Fuentes signed in 1950 with the New York Giants (one of the earliest teams to reap the bonanza of talent in the Dominican Republic), and in the same year Manolete Cáceres signed with the Detroit Tigers (although he left after less than a week at the Tigers' camp in Lakeland, Florida, citing as his reason negative attitudes toward Latinos).[83] Two more Dominicans, Ozzie Virgil and Amor Díaz, were signed in 1953; Virgil eventually became the first Dominican to play in the major leagues.

With the return of professional baseball to the Dominican Republic came the return of foreigners to Dominican teams: Puerto Ricans (Rubén Gómez), Cubans (Herberto Blanco and Gilberto Torrez), and even North Americans (Bert Haas and Bob Thurman). The number of these *importados* ranged from five to seven on a team,[84] and their presence unquestionably improved the level of play in the Dominican Republic. Similarly, Dominicans joined professional baseball teams from nearby countries in increasing numbers; many played in the Dominican Republic during the summer and abroad during the winter. In 1954, for instance, the Puerto Rican team Cangrejeros del Santurce signed three Dominicans to improve their chances for a national championship.[85]

One reason for the increased refinement of professional baseball in the 1950s was the establishment of a press corps that focused on it. Contemporary journalists such as Jorge Bornugal and others evolved a style of reportage that is peculiarly Dominican, though not without influence from other countries, especially Cuba. Rafael Rubí, a Cuban broadcaster of Dominican games, cast a long shadow. His style seemed to become incorporated into the popular lexicon as the phrases he coined were repeated by a whole generation of sportsmen and fans.[86] Television broadcasts of Dominican baseball began in 1952.[87]

Meanwhile the Dominican sports press continued to glorify Ciudad Trujillo and Santiago while slighting regional teams from the east. Chico Contón, a shortstop who played at the time, saw this as a reflection of the snobbishness of the capital, an elitism that had no place on the baseball diamond: "Yeah, we used to be attacking [baseball reporters from the capital] for this. You had to be outstanding to be recognized by them. They wrote about their people only, but we knew the good ones. Some would even say that a ball player was from the capital when he was from the [refineries of the east]."[88]

The amateur play of the 1940s had so matured and deepened the organization of baseball throughout the country that when professional baseball leagues returned in 1951, the amateur leagues were in a position to feed them. Regionales continued during this period, with large-scale tournaments in the east (around San Pedro de Macorís), in the central region (around Santiago), and near the capital. When competition ended, all-star teams from each region played against each other to determine a national champion, which then played against foreign teams. One of the most successful of these national teams was Trópico, from near San Pedro de Macorís, which won five national championships and played well in international competition.[89]

Soon the baseball played in and around San Pedro de Macorís gained recognition throughout the country and abroad. By the same token, the baseball played in Cuba and elsewhere was increasingly known in remote Dominican areas. Chico Contón has noted the impact of Cuban baseball on his refinery town of Consuelo: "Every afternoon after work we used to play against each other. I was fifteen years old then. In Consuelo, we used to listen to the Cuban ballgames: Havana, Almendares, Marianso. So each one that loves a team [in Cuba] acts like it by playing for a made up team with the name. I act like I'm on Havana. So, we make a team and play Almendares—all in Consuelo."[90]

As refinery ball—sugarball—continued to evolve its own style, those who played it were simultaneously growing more successful against outsiders: "I was born in Consuelo. Rico Carty is from there. Alfredo Griffin too. We know each other like friends . . . San Pedro area always had the good ballplayers. All of the other areas liked San Pedro players."[91] Life in the ingenio remained a struggle, and the harder it was the brighter looked the path of escape lit by baseball. Contón's description of living and playing conditions in Consuelo is remarkably similar to that of Jacobo from a decade earlier:

> In those days the wages were so low. My father was a foreman, and the wages were not good. I was born in Consuelo and went to school there, but they had a school that only went to the third grade. I said, "Well, I want an education." My grandmother lived in San Pedro, so I went there to live when I was twelve. I went to the normal school [high school]. If I stayed in Consuelo, I would not get an education. But, I'd go back and play baseball for them. I had an obligation.
>
> If you played for the team in Consuelo, you go to work like the other people, but you don't do anything. I would go to work

yeah, but the wages were so low, I said, "The hell with it! I'm not gonna work." I just walked around, and at five o'clock we go off and we practice. Nobody got money then. Strictly amateur. If we have to buy a uniform, we buy it with our own money. Our gloves? I doubt if we had nine gloves. We used to borrow each other's. We'd keep switching with the other team. If I'm playing shortstop, I leave my glove at the edge of the infield. I was sixteen then. We called it "wild ball," not educated baseball. We just throw, hit, run. We didn't have scouts, instructors. We didn't warm up. *Vamos a jugar* [let's play]. We come right from the fields into the game.[92]

In both east and west, at the professional level as well as the amateur, Dominican baseball in 1954 was becoming better organized, increasingly respected abroad, and so structured that the professional clubs regularly drew on young talent from the "wild ball" fields of the ingenios and the amateur leagues of the cities. Dominican baseball definitely possessed its own spirit, and eventually it was rewarded with the ultimate accolade: recognition from the American major leagues, which established formal ties with the Dominican leagues. This new arrangement gave unprecedented opportunities for Dominicans to play in the United States. But as we shall see in the next chapters, it proved to be a mixed blessing.

2

The Political Economy of
Dominican Baseball

● ● ● ● ● ● ● ● ●

It is impossible to discuss the political economy of Dominican baseball
without discussing Dominican relations with the United States, for these
relations underpin the entire history of economic development in the
Dominican Republic. The period since 1950 is particularly instructive.

The autonomy and cultural distinctiveness that characterized Dominican baseball from 1950 to 1954 were unique (see chapter 1). They were
certainly in contrast to the decline that marked the years 1937 to 1950,
when Dominican baseball had no organized league structure: "Sometimes they play in summer, sometimes in winter. Sometimes it was
three teams, sometimes four. If someone can pick twenty players and
pay their fees, they gonna play. Companies like Firestone, Pepsi Cola
paid . . . Here [in Santo Domingo] before 1950 they called it professional but it wasn't that kind of professional. They were professional
ballplayers but the league was not professional . . . Years ago what they
used to do, two clubs would play a twenty-one game series. If you won
eleven you were the champion . . . They were very interesting, play[ed]
real good baseball, but were not well organized."[1]

According to the most knowledgeable baseball men in the Dominican Republic, what distinguished the beisbol romantico of 1950 to
1954 from what preceded it was its organization: a league structure and
a fixed slate of games. But what distinguished beisbol romantico from
what followed was its relative autonomy: "Before 1955 [the Dominican
leagues] were not members of [North American] professional baseball.
Before 1955 they used professional players from the Dodgers, the Pirates, but they didn't have any *relationship*[2] with other major league
clubs."[3]

While this absence of a relationship was seen as a liability, it did facilitate Dominican control over most aspects of the game. By scheduling
their games in the summer to coincide with the American baseball season, Dominican baseball organizers unwittingly declared their independence by precluding the use of American players. Some American
clubs assigned players to the Dominican Republic nevertheless, and
some Americans opted on their own to play there.

1955 to 1980: The Era of Maturation

From the mid-1950s to 1980 Dominican baseball came increasingly to
depend on the American major leagues. The number of Dominicans
playing professional baseball in North America began as a trickle in the
late 1950s and early 1960s, then grew to forty-nine between 1955 and
1980 and to hundreds in the 1980s.

Two factors were responsible for this rapid growth: the forging of
"working relationships" between North American and Dominican teams,
and a change in the scheduling of the Dominican baseball season from
summer to winter. In a working relationship players and expertise were
shared by a North American team (always the senior partner that dic-
tated the terms of the relationship) and a Dominican team. The scheduling change made Dominican baseball a complement to major league
baseball rather than a competitor with it.[4]

The early successes with the San Francisco Giants of Juan Marichal
and the three Alou brothers (Jesús, Felipe, and Matty) fostered tighter
bonds between Dominicans and Americans, and with each success
came more American scouts and further movement of players. In a par-
allel development, Castro's revolution in Cuba and the subsequent em-
bargo of trade with his country by the United States cut off the major
leagues from what had been the single largest supply of talent in Latin
America, and made them focus increasingly after 1960 on the Dominican Republic.

As more Dominicans played in the United States, what had been a
sporadic flow of American players to the Dominican Republic became
institutionalized. The decision by the Dominican League of Professional Baseball to schedule its games during the winter made this possible. There was an economic incentive for Americans and Dominicans
to play winter ball, for in the days before free agency the "reserve system" kept salaries low. One all-star major leaguer from the Dominican
Republic reports having made only $6,000 in the United States in each

of his first four seasons in the 1960s. Playing winter baseball significantly supplemented this meager wage:

> In those days it was better baseball, because in those days [around
> 1961], the scouts from the United States was only Pittsburgh, Los
> Angeles, and San Francisco. The other teams didn't care about
> these Dominican players . . . All big leaguers used to play here
> in those times. We didn't make that much money as they do
> now, so we had to play here.[5]
>
> When I came here the [Licey] club in 1972 got [Steve] Yeager,
> [Steve] Garvey, [Bobby] Valentine. Monchín got some pretty
> good natives too like Teddy Martínez, J[esús] Alou. You know
> what the top salary of that group [was]? . . . Yeager was making
> $900. Garvey $1,000 . . . But they was making good money if
> you consider that their salary in the big leagues was $12,500. If
> you divide $12,500 by six months, which is the season in the
> U.S., you are making $2,000 a month and you have to pay for
> your rent, food, bills. Here, you were making $1,200 or a $1,000
> a month plus all expenses. They were making more here than in
> the States![6]

Dominican ballplayers were not motivated merely by economic gain.
To play before Dominicans was very different from playing in the
United States. Winter baseball in the Dominican Republic provided a
strong bond between these gifted, fortunate athletes and the people they
represented while in the United States; it gave them a way of showing
gratitude to the fans. Many Dominican ballplayers played at home during the winter for decades, through sickness and turmoil, whether they
were at the height of their careers or in their decline: "[My brothers and
I] used to play on the same team every year—in the outfield. Yes, I
played for Escogido every year for twenty-three years. When I was sick I
played, when I won the batting title I played. Didn't miss one."[7] This
dedication to playing at home was unweakened by a discriminatory system of wages: "We play every year here, and we do everything for the
home team. And we were the stars. But, we are getting paid much less
than Americans."[8]

The lure of cheap, abundant talent in the Dominican Republic led
American teams to establish a more substantial presence there. This was
interpreted by the Dominicans as an acknowledgment of their worth, of
the parity of their game with the American game. The bonds between
American and Dominican baseball came increasingly to resemble other
economic and political relations between the two countries. Two new
developments about 1980 brought the relations between North Ameri-

can baseball and Dominican baseball to the fore and effected a change

in the nature of baseball in the Dominican Republic.

From 1980 to the Present: The Role of Free Agency

The economic impact of free agency in the United States (begun in
1976) and the rise of the baseball academy in the Dominican Republic
brought about major changes in Dominican baseball. As the cost of
signing and re-signing American ballplayers escalated during the late
1970s, the management of various major league franchises increasingly
looked to sign young Dominicans at a fraction of the cost: "In the
United States they spend $100,000 to $150,000 signing good draft picks
out of college. Down here, I sign top players with good tools for $4,000.
Right now, the top players in the organization at Albuquerque, San Antonio, Bakersfield, and Florida are all Latino."[9] The profusion of Dominican talent is evident from the dramatic rise since around 1980 in
the number of Dominicans in the American major and minor leagues.
At the winter meetings in 1989 sixty-five Dominicans were listed as roster players out of a total of around a thousand, and some 325 Dominicans play in the minor leagues in the United States and Canada.

The growth in players' salaries in the United States since the advent
of free agency has been astronomical, a growth fueled by lucrative contracts with television networks. From 1970 to 1990 the minimum salary
for major leaguers increased from $12,000 to $125,000, or by 942 percent, and the average salary increased from $29,300 to $600,000, or by
1,948 percent. By contrast, the salary structure in Dominican baseball
has lagged far behind. The minimum salary for Americans playing in
the Dominican Republic increased from $2,100 in 1972 to $10,500
in 1989, or by 400 percent. This is hardly comparable to the increases
in the minimum and average salaries in the United States over roughly
the same period.

The disparity in salaries is aggravated by the disparity in currencies.
While Americans get paid in dollars, Dominican players get paid in
pesos. Years ago the dollar and the peso were of roughly equal value,
but now there are more than six pesos to the dollar, and yet the minimum salary for a Dominican player remains at 10,500 pesos (about
$1,700) while the minimum for an American player is $10,500. Owners of Dominican teams have traditionally underpaid their own players,
partly because they never saw them as being on a par with the Americans,[10] and partly because they could appeal to the players' nationalist
sentiments to keep down their wage demands:

The old players felt a responsibility to play. But before is not like now. Before is not really the same kind of money as now. The players wanna keep [playing] in this league, but there's no guarantees. The owners, they know you gonna play good, but they don't really care.[11]

I think owners have a lot to do with it. They treat most of the players real bad when they're young [rookies]. Then, when they get to the age they can be on their own, then [the owners] think back on what they did . . . B—— won't play here 'cause when they went to Mexico City [for the Caribbean Series], the owners offer us $2,000 to win the whole thing. Then we win the whole thing and we get back and only get paid $600.[12]

Dominican players have traditionally seen the chance to play in their country as a way of expressing solidarity with their compatriots, particularly for those who play in their home town. But Dominicans playing in the United States have benefited from the same escalating salaries as their American teammates have, and as a result they have chosen in increasing numbers not to play in their homeland, with disastrous results for Dominican baseball (see chapter 3).

Of course not all Dominican players refuse to play in their own country, and of those who do even the most successful often remember their less gifted and less fortunate countrymen and earn the gratitude and loyalty of their fans. The retired pitcher Joaquín Andujar offers a case in point. Known in the United States for his hotheadedness, Andujar has given tirelessly to the poor in his community.[13] In response the people of San Pedro de Macorís treat any affront to him as an affront to them all. When Andujar was pitching one winter for San Pedro, his manager moved to take him out of a game after a particularly rough outing. Andujar objected strenuously in front of the fans, but relented and marched back to the dugout. After the game the fans waited for the manager in the parking lot of the stadium and threw stones at his car. When in the winter of 1987 Andujar first contemplated retirement from the game, the people of San Pedro de Macorís gave him a sumptuous dinner and implored him to reconsider.[14] Andujar stopped pitching in the Dominican league some time ago, but his charitable works and his efforts to develop local talent continue.

The crisis in Dominican baseball caused by free agency in the United States has had an interesting effect: the association for professional Dominican players is now also struggling for free agency. This is sure to have an impact on the way Dominican baseball is organized.

Dominican baseball is separated along traditional lines of professional and amateur, and for years before the present era professional teams looked to the best amateurs and to professionals in other countries to fill their rosters.

The number of professional baseball teams in the Dominican Republic was at first two, is now six, and may soon be eight.[15] The teams represent the largest cities in the country: the capital, Santo Domingo, has two (Tigres del Licey and Leones del Escogido), and there is one team in each of the four cities San Pedro de Macorís (Estrellas Orientales), Santiago (Aguilas del Cibao), La Romana (Azucareros del Este), and San Cristóbal (Caimanes del Sur).

With the exception of Licey, which is a cooperative, the teams are privately held. All teams play a sixty-game schedule beginning in late October and ending in February. The season culminates in a round-robin playoff, the two finalists of which play in the Caribbean Series against the champions of Mexico, Venezuela, and Puerto Rico.

Dominican clubs sign Dominican players if they are available, and American players if they are eligible and affordable. An American player's eligibility is determined by the amount of time he has spent in the major leagues; the formula is spelled out for each Dominican team in its working agreement with its American parent: "If you know what you're doing, you get a good relationship with [some team] in the United States, or a working agreement. The Aguilas club got a working agreement with Pittsburgh for twenty years, and they won a lotta pennants because all the ballplayers from Pittsburgh come to play for the Aguilas."[16]

American players, known as importados, can play in the Dominican Republic only under certain conditions: "If you pitch more than one hundred innings or bat more than two hundred fifty at bats and play more than two years in the big leagues, you cannot play. If you are a native it is okay."[17]

While there are no restrictions on the rights of Dominican players to sign with a local club, the reserve system is in effect in the Dominican Republic, which means that players are signed and released only at the behest of their club. Dominicans are typically signed as they come up through the amateur ranks or through the professional rookie leagues (a recent invention). Once signed by a professional team a Dominican player belongs to it until he retires or the club trades him. North American players are not subject to this system.

Under a working agreement, which can be either formal or semiformal, a major league club makes available as many as six of its players at a time to its Dominican partner. These players are usually young and in need of experience, and although they cannot be coerced to play by their American club they are strongly encouraged to do so to hone their skills or as part of their rehabilitation from injury. For their part, Dominican clubs are subject to certain requirements: their facilities must meet major league specifications, and their salaries must conform with basic guidelines.

A working relationship gives a North American club a Dominican spokesperson, a liaison to represent its interests. The Dominican partner can also provide valuable information by scouting promising talent and protecting unsigned prospects from other scouts. The major league team I worked with most closely negotiated with its Dominican partner about who the manager, pitching coach, and trainer of the Dominican affiliate would be. At times the murky ties between North American and Dominican teams have allowed for abuses. One major league club found that the owner of its Dominican team, authorized by the North American parent club to scout and sign players on its behalf at a bonus of $4,000, was instead signing young Dominicans to a bonus of 4,000 pesos and keeping the difference.

Professional Dominican Players

The Federación Nacional de Peloteros Profesionales (FENAPEPRO) is an association of professional Dominican players led by a president and a full complement of officers. Its members pay $50 a year in dues and number about four hundred, of which some 150 have played in the United States. The rest have played only in the Dominican Republic and include walk-ons (players with only brief experience), rookies, and reserves.

The president of FENAPEPRO is responsible for canvassing the members to determine their needs and to press the owners on their behalf. The organization is also able to order strikes, which it has done on occasion for a day or two. (Like their counterparts in the United States, Dominican players are concerned mainly with wages, medical insurance, and pensions.) And FENAPEPRO represents its members in legal disputes ranging from paternity suits to litigation with American franchises over unpaid bonuses.

In the 1980s FENAPEPRO took on the thorny issue of free agency. Many people at the upper echelons of the sport feel that the organization is too weak to force the issue:

[FENAPEPRO is] weak. I don't think this free agency is going to work now. I don't know about later. They're weak and need to gain the respect of everybody; respect from the league, respect from the fans. The league gives them the job of preparing the all star game. Every year is a failure. They are disorganized.[18]

FENAPEPRO wants only for itself, to justify its position. They can't get the players together. The owners are too strong and they are with each other [united].[19]

Most players, on the other hand, feel strongly that free agency is feasible and would provide badly needed security:

Gerónimo [president of FENAPEPRO until 1989] is doin' a big time job, big time! We got everything we need in this league—respect! The owners think they got the person, they got everything. It's not fair. They been doin' that long enough already . . . Here we're trying to protect ourselves and make sure a young guy gets what he deserves. When I was in my rookie year I was pitching every day, and I was makin' 150 pesos a month. And I ask for a 50 peso raise in the last month of the season, and they told me no!"[20]

If we get free agency like in the States its gonna be a lotta good things. I would like to stay at home and play in La Romana, and I could if we had free agency.[21]

Some players are concerned that free agency is unworkable because they believe the owners are stronger than the union and would be able to break it. This is because each team keeps a large number of reserve players and can use them as a weapon. There is a concern that in the event of a strike the reserves will break from the union and be used as scabs: "If we give them trouble, they will bring in the junk players."[22] Ironically, one argument against free agency made by a powerful foe addresses this same point from a different perspective: "Cut the roster to thirty players and ten reserves. Licey pays each month 90,000 pesos, 270,000 pesos in a season to reserves. Escogido, too. They got maybe 130 reserves eatin' up the money. Cut them, and give more money to the players. Open it up to Americans, too. If Hershiser [the star pitcher for the Los Angeles Dodgers, ineligible according to Dominican rules] wanna play, let him play."[23]

One of the most sensitive issues in Dominican baseball is the discrepancy in pay between American and Dominican players, a discrepancy magnified by the declining value of the peso. For Dominicans, to be perceived as unworthy of equal wages at home when they have already achieved them in the United States is the final insult. Moreover the owners cannot plead poverty (nor have they), for the government partially subsidizes their efforts to lure American players to the Dominican Republic: an owner need pay an American player only the minimum amount he would pay a Dominican (10,500 pesos) and the Dominican Secretariat for Sports pays the difference between this and the minimum salary for an American ($10,500). These inequities make it difficult for established Dominicans to play and onerous for those who do to continue playing. The players are turning increasingly to FENAPEPRO for solutions.

From Blackcatchers to Baseball Academies

Intense competition among the major league teams for the best Dominican talent began in earnest around 1980. Before then only a few teams like Pittsburgh, Toronto, Los Angeles, and San Francisco had been interested. Soon there were full-time scouts from every team, who scoured the country in search of native talent. One reads about the really fine scouts, such as the Dodgers' Ralph Avila and the Blue Jays' Epy Guerrero, but most scouts were less committed to their charges. In the years before legislation that controlled them, these scouts could be rapacious: lying to parents and prospects alike, cheating them, in some cases sequestering them. Their techniques were so reminiscent of those of the West African slave traders of three centuries earlier that I facetiously refer to these unscrupulous scouts as "blackcatchers."

The free-roving scouts of the 1970s gave way to baseball academies— full-time facilities for producing baseball talent. The academies made the process of securing talent grow less brigandish, more routinized, and more civilized. They are the latest manifestation of a process that has been unfolding for more than thirty years, and they are central to the future of Dominican baseball.

The academy is the baseball counterpart of the colonial outpost, the physical embodiment overseas of the parent franchise. It operates more or less like the subsidiary of any other foreign company: it finds raw materials (talented athletes), refines them (trains the athletes), and ships abroad finished products (baseball players). There are thirteen academies across the country, ranging from the seasonal and poorly equipped to the year-round and well equipped.

The first academy was built just north of Santo Domingo by the Toronto Blue Jays. Their director of scouting in the country, Epy Guerrero, decided in 1977 to build a compound where he could better observe and monitor the young athletes in his charge. Soon after, the par-

ent organization decided to fund a much larger project, one costing
$150,000 a year. This new project included a playing field and a
dormitory.

The most elaborate of the academies is Campo Las Palmas, the Los
Angeles Dodgers' sprawling compound east of Santo Domingo. Carved
out of the surrounding sugar cane fields, it includes two major league
baseball diamonds and has complete facilities and staff. Other clubs are
more modest. Some house their charges in urban guest homes, and until recently one club simply used cots under the stadium grandstand.

All the academies are required to comply with guidelines laid down
by the Dominican government. Before the government intervened
abuses were rampant: academies signed as many players as possible
(some as young as thirteen) and separated them from their families without any consideration of the consequences, hid the boys so that other
scouts would not get hold of them, and failed to pay bonuses that were
promised.[24] Appalled at the way scouts were treating Dominican youth,
President Hugo Blanco issued Presidential Decree 3450 in 1984. Under
this decree all scouts operating in the country had to be registered with
the Dominican baseball commissioner, and all minor league contracts
signed in the country had to be approved by the government.[25] No one
under seventeen could be signed to a professional contract (a similar
rule was put into effect in 1984 by the commissioner of major league
baseball in the United States), and English classes were compulsory for
all players in the Dominican Republic. The changes did much to protect young Dominican athletes from the more rapacious scouts and organizations. The baseball franchises that had been more heavily involved in the country welcomed the new rules, since they had already
done more than comply with them. The more slipshod baseball operations were the ones to feel the brunt of the rules.

Gaining entrance to the academy follows a fairly standard routine (see
chapter 3). Tryouts are announced in local newspapers or privately arranged, and young men come to camp on any morning. Most hopefuls
try out at the suggestion of a scout affiliated with the camp, but others
try out on their own. Prospects are quickly screened, and those accepted
are brought in for a thirty-day evaluation, during which time they are
evaluated both physically and emotionally and taught baseball skills.
This is a new experience for the boys and causes much anxiety for them
(see chapter 4). At the end of the month the staff must decide whether to
extend contracts to the boys. The lucky ones are signed on as rookies for
bonuses of around $4,000; the others are released and sent back to their
families, but they can reapply to the academy after thirty days.

A newly signed player is no longer an amateur; he has become a professional. The rookie is expected to play with young players from other academies in a summer rookie league, and in a winter rookie league that same year. Both rookie leagues are affiliated with the American minor league system. During the summer season, which lasts three months, the boys are paid by the American parent team that signed them (which also pays the salaries of the manager and staff); in the winter they are paid by the Dominican affiliate. Salaries are based on seniority: first-year players earn $700 a month, second-year players $800 a month, and third-year players $900 a month. After three years a player is either advanced to a higher league or released.

Amateur Baseball

A country that produces as many professional ballplayers as the Dominican Republic does needs to have well-organized amateur baseball. In addition to leagues in which schools play, there is a very well run league for the armed forces. Most amateur baseball is played in hundreds of locally organized amateur leagues, where most of the young players who go on to play professionally begin their careers. The structure of the league is fairly straightforward. Teams are generally organized by entrepreneurs, politicians, ballplayers, and other people who want to make a name for themselves. Each of the twenty-six provinces in the Dominican Republic has a baseball association that oversees amateur play, and together the twenty-six associations make up the Amateur Baseball Federation, which is in charge of the juvenile program. All children under eighteen who play amateur baseball belong to this program, which is known as class A. Players in class A are divided up by age until they are thirteen; from then until they are eighteen they play together, at the highest level of the program. If a player is good enough he can join the class AA program, which has no age limits, but once he has played at that level he can never return to class A.

Obviously the class AA program is more competitive and has traditionally groomed the best players. As in the United States, many of the best amateurs go on to sign professional contracts.

The Dominican government plays a substantial role in subsidizing amateur baseball. Tax money supports the various federations around the country, as well as such ancillary services as buses, parks, and lights. Money is paid to at least 350 people who are supposed to instruct young players in the amateur leagues. Since getting into the class A and class AA programs depends largely on individual initiative and patronage, and government subsidies are granted to the league founders, the programs need to be regularly monitored and evaluated so that the nepotism so

endemic in Dominican life does not take hold. From all I was able to gather, oversight is woefully inept and the source of a good deal of criticism by high-ranking members of the baseball community: "Blame it on the poor program they got because everyone wants to collect money, and no one wanna instruct the kids. The government got about 350 persons collecting a check every month from the secretary of sports—instructors. And nobody works. If you got connections, if you are president of that Amateur Baseball Federation you gonna receive a check as an instructor, but you're not gonna help a kid." [26]

I spent time in one of the most traditional amateur belts: the area around San Pedro de Macorís where the refineries are situated. There refinery teams such as Quisqueya, Porvenir, and Consuelo continually play each other. Their games are still highly regarded and have often launched professional careers (although there are other options now and amateur play elsewhere competes favorably with that of the refinery teams). It is in the ramshackle baseball parks with makeshift grandstands that some of the really wild and woolly baseball is played. The stands are filled with cane cutters ready to enjoy a bit of life after a day or week of back-breaking work. The players are striving both to win for their ingenio and to attract the attention of some North American scout. They assume that any man who looks like an Anglo must work for a major league franchise. Scouts do come to these highly touted contests between refineries: two men were signed by scouts from Oakland and Los Angeles in the very first game I attended. The teams were once made up of cane cutters residing at the refineries, but now the managers sign players from elsewhere based on their skill and reputation. Strictly speaking, the players for these refinery teams are not amateurs. They fall rather in the gray area of semiprofessionals, for they get paid a small fee to play for the company. Much of the best "amateur baseball" is organized this way.

Amateur baseball in the Dominican Republic has been weakened by many changes, of which the most recent is the forging of links between the professional Dominican leagues and the academies. The Dominican teams see it as being in their best interests to help subsidize the academies and develop good relations with the players who attend them, since it is from the academies that most of their players are now signed. Additionally, the directors of the academies and the owners of the teams often form close associations, which makes it likely that players from a given academy will end up with a certain team. All this makes for stronger ties between the academy and professional Dominican teams and helps to eclipse amateur baseball.

While the organization of Dominican baseball in some ways resembles strongly the way baseball is organized in the United States, there are important differences. Some of these are due to the general dependence of Dominican baseball teams on their corporate parents, and others to the presence of strong, uniquely Dominican cultural structures (see chapters 5 and 6).

The Determinators

The Underdevelopment
of Dominican Baseball

● ● ● ● ● ● ● ●

In the long run, to mine the baseball riches of the Dominican Republic
will impoverish the Dominican game, for the country's supply of baseball talent is not inexhaustible. Not only is amateur baseball being evis-
cerated by the academies, but the professional winter league teams are
increasingly dependent on American major league teams. At the same
time successful players returning from play in the United States are increasingly reluctant to play in the winter league—this strikes a devastat-
ing blow to the integrity and health of Dominican baseball. The effects
of these trends are already being felt, as attendance is falling off at parks
around the country.

The Impact of the Academy

The physical and organizational presence of baseball academies run by
major league franchises in the Dominican Republic has fundamentally
undermined the long-standing sovereignty of Dominican baseball. First,
the academies have undercut the traditional role of professional Dominican teams in locating talent (especially so because the academies
are always present), and the Dominican teams are unable to protect
their prospects from incursions by American teams. Second, the academies blur the boundary between professionals and amateurs by allow-
ing them to coexist during the monthlong periods when signed and
unsigned live and play side by side. Third and most important, the

academies contribute to the cannibalization of the Dominican amateur leagues. By signing players at the age of seventeen and courting them even earlier, the academies are weakening the upper echelons of amateur baseball.[1] The academies have direct access to unsigned talent and can bypass the amateur leagues entirely.

But the amateur leagues may not be the helpless though honorable victims of American expansionism that they seem to be. Pragmatists point to the desperate poverty of so many prospects as the main reason why talent circumvents amateur baseball wherever it can: "Yes, the problem is that we are a poor country, and we need the dollars. You can't say to a boy whose father is poor, 'Hey, don't sign so quickly.' You can't do that because you are killing that boy. He doesn't have any other chance like this."[2] Increasingly, there have been charges of massive corruption and commercialism at all levels of amateur baseball.[3] One former director of an amateur baseball club who asked to remain anonymous believes that amateur baseball is a victim of its own greed: it abrogated many of its responsibilities, and the academies assumed them.

> Twenty years ago television was zero in this country. You got Colgate, Marlboro, big companies. They got money to spend on publicity and promotion. The best way to get publicity every Monday morning was to have an amateur team . . . At that time the company spent that money because they can't spend the money on T.V. ads. For example, we got a company named Maprica fifteen years ago. [It] was a furniture company. They start[ed] with a very poor club. They wanna be involved in amateur level because the only thing you see is not that Maprica got beat, but Maprica's name was there.
>
> Now all the big companies don't spend a penny on amateur baseball because to receive good publicity now you have to have a good ball club. No one wants to sponsor a poor club. Why should they spend $3,000 to sponsor a poor club when they can put it into T.V. ads? They want winning clubs only. In the past they don't care whether it was positive or negative. Now they want only good players and they pay. Now they got only four or five good clubs where they used to have twenty. Where [does] the kid coming from the class A program [eighteen years old and younger] go to? [Now] they don't have the chance to play in AA 'cause [the sponsors] want experienced amateur players to win a pennant and receive good publicity. Thousands of kids coming from the class A program don't have any place to play. They got three choices: come to the academy, go to another sport, or go to the Malecón and sell drugs.[4]

This is only one interpretation of the cause; there is no disputing the   **49**
effect, which is a significant weakening by the academies of the amateur   *The*
leagues. If one believes that local control over the development of Do-   *Determinators*
minican talent is preferable to foreign control, this erosion is a problem.

The Increasing Dependency of Dominican Baseball

While the relationship between Dominican and American professional
baseball has been recognized for more than thirty years, the tendency of
American baseball to hinder the Dominican game is comparatively recent. American baseball teams have exerted their control chiefly by des-
ignating which players should go to the Dominican Republic, and by
providing instructional and managerial staff. A team can of course assist
the cross-cultural transmission of baseball rather than hamper it. The
Los Angeles Dodgers have been exceptionally sensitive to Latin American operations and culture: they have urged their staff to get bilingual
training,[5] and each spring at their camp in Vero Beach they offer Spanish classes for English speakers and English classes for Spanish speakers.
Their manager, Tom Lasorda, gained extensive experience managing
local teams in the 1960s in the Caribbean.

Not all organizations are so enlightened, however. One American
manager, assigned by his parent club to manage a Dominican team, ran
afoul of the cultural sensitivities of his Dominican players. For instance, rather than ease up on his American notions of punctuality he
insisted on disciplining players who showed up late for practice; he had
failed to learn that punctuality is a culturally variable concept. Although he has the most talented ball club in the league, his players performed very poorly. One long-time baseball administrator in Santo Domingo has likened Dominican players in their own country not to
people at work but to people who have come home from work. At work
one has to be punctual and live by restrictive rules, but at home one can
relax and be somewhat looser. Dominican players insist on having
things a bit more lax than in the United States, and expect to be treated
more leniently. An organization that is culturally invested in the Dominican Republic will seek to have its people fit the Dominican system
rather than try to make the system fit its people.

Another way American teams have hurt professional Dominican
baseball is by pressuring well-paid Dominican players under contract to
them to forgo playing in the Dominican Republic. Because of the mul-
tiyear contracts and high salaries that so many major leaguers have,
their teams do not want them to risk injury. An American team can
make life so difficult for a player that he will leave the Dominican team

prematurely. There are many cases of Dominican and American players who have left their team before the championship series or even after
only a few games. The press will of course play up these situations in the
hopes of incensing the fans, as the Santo Domingo daily paper *Listin
diario* did when it ran the screaming headline "Cincinnati Prohibits
Rijo from Pitching" before a championship series.[6] Because of the increasing power of American teams and the rapidly escalating salaries of
players, the fans are easily provoked.

The reason for the diminishing interest of Dominican stars in winter
ball is simple: the risk of an injury that would end their career is too
great and the pay too low. Dominican players like Tony Fernández,
George Bell, Pedro Guerrero, and others earn in the vicinity of two million dollars a year. An article in *Listin diario* on 4 April 1988 boasted
that the thirty-four Dominicans who played on opening day of 1988
collectively earned $15,484,000 for the season.[7] These figures have
surged since then, making the salaries paid by owners of Dominican
teams amount to nothing by comparison.

Almost everyone I interviewed in the Dominican Republic agreed
that players are reluctant to risk future earnings in the light of the salaries that free agency has brought them:

> [The big salaried players] don't care. Cesarín [Gerónimo], Mari-
> chal and them, they used to play alla time. Now it's big money
> and the guys don't wanna [play].[8]

> It's not a lotta competition like there was before. Then, there was
> a lotta big league players, natives. I keep playing 'cause I wanna
> be a better pitcher. Another guy makes decent money in the
> States; you know, guaranteed contract. And here, I don't think
> the owners gonna pay that kinda money.[9]

> The big money is a big part of it too, but most of us are afraid of
> getting hurt. You taking every risk and losing all the money.[10]

> Well, we're working on a big one-year deal. It will be my last year
> here 'cause I'm headin' for the thirties you know. I'm twenty-nine
> now and pitchin' so much . . . but its not gonna help me with
> spring training in the States.[11]

Not only do most of the "big money" players no longer play because
of covert pressure from their clubs, but those who do play often do so in
a token way. In the words of one retired player, now a scout: "I don't
care to manage [one of the Dominican professional teams] here. The
players make too much money, so you can't get them to do anything.

A—— would never pitch when I needed him. [He would say,] 'Mario, I'm sick!' They would go drinking all night and couldn't play for us. American players too."[12]

Dominican fans and the press view this attitude as a betrayal, a lack of respect on the part of their more talented and fortunate countrymen. Retired Dominican players who played through the lean years of the reserve system also resent the reluctance of Dominican major leaguers to play winter ball: "Everybody recognized us then because we were in the papers every day. A lotta people don't like G—— [a current player] because he doesn't play here. They are baseball fans. That's why they don't like these guys that come here and don't play ball. They used to like me because I came and played. Sometimes they see G—— don't go to the park, but they see him in a discothèque dancing and they get angry."[13]

Intensified International Competition

The intensified presence of the United States has brought international attention to the Dominican Republic. Other nations where baseball is being played have begun to look at Latin America as a source of talent. Now that baseball is an Olympic sport the Soviet Union has called on its socialist partner, Cuba, to teach it to its young athletes. In the Dominican Republic the Japanese have recently entered the fray; surely this means that baseball prospects in the Dominican Republic will take part in international competition. The Hiroshima Carp of Japan have bought land outside San Pedro de Macorís and are preparing to invest a substantial sum in the development of an academy (several million dollars, according to rumor). The director of the Los Angeles Dodgers' Latin American operations, Ralph Avila, has pointed out that the Japanese have been attending spring training in Florida for years, so he was not surprised to see them at Campo Las Palmas. Nevertheless, their rumored attempt to buy a rather large share in the Dominican professional team the Estrellas Orientales is a different and more significant matter.

The Hiroshima team is undoubtedly the first of many, and the mining of Dominican players will only intensify in such a climate. A senior sportswriter in Santo Domingo felt certain that "in five years the Japanese will compete with the United States in this country."[14] When I asked Dominican players in the winter league what their perceptions were of these developments, they were overwhelmingly enthusiastic and hopeful for greater opportunity:

I think its a good idea if the Japanese come. It's a lotta guys with a lotta talent. They get fired from the States, they still can play and make a living.[15]

Yeah, I think it's great. It brings more work for the people, and dollars for the Dominican Republic.[16]

Salaries go up, but its gonna mean more people [are] enthusiastic for the game, and the fans will come back.[17]

At least one reputable source said the Japanese would not make serious inroads into Dominican baseball: "Well, they need ballplayers. But the Latin players, they don't like Japan very much. The language, the customs, and they have to practice [too hard]. I have been talking to Dominicans that went there. If they have a choice, they choose the U.S. [The Japanese] can have some boys, maybe the ones that we can't sell to the U.S., they go to Japan."[18]

During one field trip to Santo Domingo in early 1989 I had ample opportunity to watch a Japanese film crew (from NHK, the Japan Broadcasting Corporation) working on what was to be a one-hour special for Japanese television. For six straight weeks, eight to ten hours a day, they filmed young prospects in every phase of life at the academy: getting medical examinations, signing contracts, taking part in practice and instruction, and living in the dormitories. When I spoke with members of the crew they had shot more than eighty cans of film and countless hours of videotape—far more than would be needed for a one-hour special. In response to my question the producer denied that the amount of footage was excessive: he wanted to be sure of everything. But when I asked what would be done with the footage not used the producer admitted that it would be available for "other uses." He was vague about whether these included uses by Japanese teams, but he seemed not to reject the possibility.

To Americans long used to having free rein in the Dominican Republic, the presence of a Japanese company interested in baseball but unaffiliated with any team anywhere is more ominous. Such a presence became a possibility when representatives of a Japanese firm approached the director of the Los Angeles Dodgers' camp to see if he would help them start an academy.[19] When asked why a firm unaffiliated with professional baseball would want to do such a thing, they replied that they wanted to produce players for sale on the world market. The Dominican Republic, so rich in baseball talent, seemed a logical place to set up this operation, a sort of ballplayer factory. Korea, Taiwan, Australia, and other countries have already developed their own brands of professional baseball and will step up their programs, especially now that baseball is a worldwide sport. Should these countries hatch plans similar to those of the Japanese, there could be grave implications for American teams and Dominican players.

Scouting and Signing Irregularities

The presence in the Dominican Republic of roughly thirteen academies and scouts from all the franchises in the country heightens the competition for talent. Presidential decrees and rulings from the commissioner notwithstanding, overzealous scouts and perfunctory academies continue to commit occasional improprieties. The prevailing attitude is that the ends justify the means: to put the entire baseball system in jeopardy by engaging in dubious practices may be unfortunate, but warranted because it provides a few young men with the fame and riches the entire country seems to be after.

The competition to sign players often leads scouts to exaggerate and at times to lie outright. Stories of scouts signing players right under the noses of other scouts are part of the baseball folklore of the Dominican Republic. The stories provoke laughter, but the practice prompts guardedness and resentment:

> We'll continue to sign players without a camp [academy]. We signed a player out of the Yankees camp in November. The Yankees raised hell about it. But what could they do? They still hadn't signed the boy.[20]

> Scouts are involved in stealing each other's players. A—— wanted me to take him to Campo Las Palmas the next time I went. I asked him about stealing other players [I suspected his motives]. He told me that a guy will pull the young men over to the side and ask, "How long you been here?" Whatever the reply, he will continue, "What? And they haven't signed you? We'll do it right now."[21]

> I had to chase two scouts away from my camp last month. They came to my camp during our lunch break and took two of my players to the other side of the stadium. I caught those guys and told them to leave.[22]

To protect themselves against these abuses, many academies often hide their prospects, bringing forth charges of kidnaping. Papi Bisono, former commissioner of Dominican baseball, recalls one mother who looked for her missing son: "She'd heard that her son had been taken away by a baseball scout and asked me if I could help find him. And this was one of many complaints that I received about these camps. The scouts who ran these camps had these kids hidden; that is the real truth. These camps were hideouts because the scouts didn't want their kids seen by other scouts. It almost seemed like they were concentration camps."[22]

Many of these abuses have been corrected, but others have not. At the time of my interview with him, one official was investigating allegations that scouts had signed players for one amount and paid them only a fraction of it. In some instances there was no delivery at all of the money that had been promised. Cheating young hopefuls out of their due continues despite decrees against it. One scout confided that if the government blocks his signing of a young player, he will simply circumvent the ruling by saying that the boy was signed in Haiti. Some teams even get their way by threatening to leave the country if they are interfered with by the government.[24]

All this maneuvering may have driven the fans away in the past few years. When I visited the Dominican Republic in the winter of 1988–89, everyone I spoke to suggested that attendance at the country's premier facility, Estadio Quisqueya, was down from the preceding year (this was confirmed by my own observations).

In my last field trip (January–February 1989) declining attendance had certainly become an issue for those connected to Dominican baseball. The press and owners were mulling over the possible reasons why the fans were staying away in such numbers. Monchín Pichardo, president of Licey, provoked a controversy when he suggested that because of the fans' declining interest the League needed a *descanso* (rest). A very sensitive chord had been struck, and the sports pages of the dailies were filled with editorials and statements opposing the plan. Referring to the owner of San Pedro's team, the title of one article read, "Antún Opposes League Recess."[25] Next to this was another article proclaiming the strength of Dominican baseball, "Griffin Thinks Dominican Baseball Ought to Recover Its Force,"[26] in which the writer articulated simultaneously the fear that baseball was in crisis and the hope of unlimited potential: "Those boys will be in charge of the return of the fans to the baseball parks because, with total assurance they are the future stars of Dominican baseball . . . Griffin reminds us that the fans have to back these young players because the big league figures who have multiple-year contracts continue to refuse playing in their country."[27]

All whom I interviewed—fans, players, journalists, and administrators—acknowledged the problem but assigned different causes to it:

[Pichardo] wants a "rest" because Gerónimo [president of
FENAPEPRO] is pushing for free agency. It's a lockout, pure and
simple.[28]

Used to be seventy-five centavos in the bleachers, now it's two
pesos, sometimes five pesos. Who can come?[29]

Another part of it is that they are afraid to leave their homes.
Without no lights, you know, *apagones* [blackouts]. It's a big part
of it. Transportation too. It's hard for them at eleven o'clock to
find a bus and they don't have that much money for a cab.[30]

Others suggested to me that the declining attendance was caused by
the deteriorating facilities in the ballpark, the refusal of players to appear
in the Dominican winter league, the absence of promotions, and the
less than adequate press coverage. Clearly there is a genuine crisis in
Dominican baseball, a direct result of the success of Dominicans in the
game and of the American effort to exploit it. The background to these
developments is the larger relationship between the United States and
the Dominican Republic, which must be examined critically.

Dependency and Baseball:
Camps, Cramps, and Visa Stamps

Andre Gunder Frank was among the first to explore the impact of colonialism in Latin America from a perspective focusing on dependency.[31]
In his view the relation between colonialist nation (core) and colony
(periphery) is one of simultaneous development and underdevelopment. The core nation expropriates the colony's resources and imports
them for processing and manufacture. Finished products are consumed
in the home market as well as reexported to the colony. This dynamic
results in the enrichment of the core and the impoverishment of the
periphery. The system is often guaranteed at first by a direct military
presence; in a neocolonial setting it can usually be sustained simply by
the threat of force and the political and economic power of the multinational, as it is in the Dominican Republic. The same principles can be
seen operating in the world of baseball.

More recent studies of neocolonialism have focused on the means by
which manufacturing (and hence labor) moves away from the core and
toward the periphery. Lured by a cheap and docile labor force, corporations based in industrial countries move their manufacturing plants offshore. This process, which has been called the international division of

labor,[32] is bringing about a major change in contemporary capitalism. A fitting example of the process in the Dominican Republic is provided by the many *zonas francas* (free zones) that are springing up all over the country. Begun as part of President Reagan's Caribbean Basin Initiative, the zonas francas are manufacturing enclaves built by the Dominican government. Foreign manufacturers (usually small to medium-sized) are lured there with the promise of cheap and plentiful labor. The political economy of Dominican baseball is to some extent comparable, since young Dominican ballplayers do provide cheap labor. But although Dominican ballplayers may be signed cheaply, once they go to the United States they become highly skilled and incredibly well paid. Rather than suffer exploitation, Dominican ballplayers frequently retire as very rich men.

The competition among American teams to sign as many players as possible is intense and often wasteful. There are fifty Dominicans out of 170 players in the minor league operations of the Oakland Athletics; the team signed thirty Dominicans between December 1987 and March 1988 alone. In the United States this northward movement of Latino ballplayers is periodically construed as a flooding of the baseball market with cheap foreign talent. Traditionally the government has come to the aid of threatened industries by imposing tariffs or outright limits on foreign products and labor. On occasion limits have been applied to Dominican ballplayers.

In 1986 there were 956 major league players, of whom 102 were foreign. Almost all the foreigners were Hispanic (ninety-nine), and forty-five of them were Dominican. Although the U.S. Department of Labor does not impose quotas on foreign players in the major leagues, the quota that it does impose on the minor leagues affects the majors indirectly. Only 10 percent of minor league players can be foreign, which translates into roughly 520 visas for foreign players. Teams do all they can to get around the quotas: "If some teams had their way they'd [each] be signing 50 or 60 Latins."[33] The Montreal Expos and the Toronto Blue Jays, which are among the most active teams in the Dominican Republic, have most of their minor league teams in Canada and until recently were not subject to the quotas. All major league teams have recourse to a Dominican rookie league that is affiliated with the American minor league system and that is also exempt; they scout and sign players in this league and bring to the United States only those ballplayers who are qualified.

Until 1989 the total number of visas allowed by the U.S. Department of Labor for minor league players was allocated to each major league parent club by the commissioner of baseball. The allocation was some-

what uneven: teams that were more active in recruiting Latin players
were given more visas, and teams that were less active could trade their visas to other teams in return for favors. In 1989 the rules were changed: each club is now allotted twenty-four visas, which are not transferable.

The quota system is a response by the U.S. Immigration and Naturalization Service, the U.S. Department of Labor, and the baseball commissioner's office to the competition between clubs for foreign talent and the potential inundation of the United States by Latino players.[34] The rules governing the granting of work visas to foreign nationals stipulate that the work must be of a kind that cannot be performed by Americans. This restriction derives from the protectionist impulse of the market and from fears of national vulnerability. These feelings are heightened as baseballs are stitched in Haiti, aluminum bats are produced in Japan, mitts are made in Taiwan, and players are increasingly coming from Latin America. The internationalization of baseball contributes to the perception that the American pastime is moving offshore.

The response of each American club to these protectionist measures depends on how heavily the club is invested in the Dominican Republic (and other Latin American countries). Teams that have a substantial head start in the Dominican Republic and elsewhere and have mined most of the talent are at odds with the government's restrictive visa policies; less active franchises in Latin America favor the policies because they curb the competition. In looking at multinational corporations, Barnet and Müller have demonstrated that nationalist considerations are superseded by the internationalism of contemporary production;[35] protectionist measures impede or serve a firm depending on whether they help maximize its profits. A major league franchise is not a multinational firm in the strict sense of the term, but it does resemble one in some respects. Because of the international nature of modern baseball, a team finds itself periodically bridling under the constraints imposed by the governments of the United States and the Dominican Republic. Each government seeks to protect what it perceives as a national treasure—baseball—against a system of production that is increasingly international.

Underdeveloping Dominican Baseball

In assessing the impact of the United States on Dominican baseball, it is essential to distinguish the various levels: individual, institutional, and cultural. A failure to do so causes a good deal of confusion over whether

Dominican players are exploited and whether the presence and growing interference of the United States in Dominican baseball and culture helps or hinders the game and society as a whole.

At the individual level the strongest force in the Dominican Republic is a pervasive poverty, which ensnares most Dominicans and deprives them of economic opportunity. The prospects for improving the lot of the Dominicans seem even bleaker when one realizes how few children attend school: at just about any time of day one can find school-age children playing baseball instead. Education and occupational preparation have nothing to offer those who need it, so there is no correlation between education and employment.[36] Many Dominican boys see baseball as their only escape, and the inordinate pull of the sport over them is strengthened by the astounding success that the best Dominican players have achieved in North American professional baseball.

Most Dominicans see their alternatives as sugar cane and baseball, and the choice is obvious: there are no cultural heroes with a machete in their hand. This was made clear in a tragicomic way in the early 1980s, when the Dominican government closed its border with Haiti (as it does periodically when nationalist sentiment and hatred of the Haitians grow strong enough). This had immediate implications for the Dominican economy, since more than 70 percent of the agricultural work force is Haitian—a sad but telling fact. The sugar cane had to be harvested, and a group of famous baseball players led by a retired major leaguer formed a movement to mobilize people by appealing to their patriotism. The plan was for all Dominicans to roll up their sleeves and harvest the cane themselves, led by the baseball notables and aided by generous press coverage. When it came time to begin the "people's cane harvest," television cameras were ready and thousands of people gathered at the scene. The crowd parted as the ballplayers arrived in work clothes, ready for their Sisyphean task. The cameras rolled as they hacked away at the cane, which soon formed a string of piles. But no one made a move to help the players: instead the crowd stood incredulous, laughing because men so rich and talented were performing such a task. After a few hours the players surrendered to the cane field, emerging thirsty, sweaty, and bloodied. Cane, as they all knew, is really no alternative to baseball. This episode was a pungent reminder of how true this is, one that could not escape the youth of the Dominican Republic—just as the mansions and expensive cars of Dominican star athletes are tangible reminders of what most Dominican boys feel can be theirs if they work hard and get a break.

The dream of success at baseball is elemental, and success is broadly defined. Even Dominican players who fail to reach the major leagues and play instead in American minor league cities are considered finan-

cially successful, and those who remain in the baseball academies for
two years and do not play in North America at all still earn more money
than they would in a decade on the streets or in the cane fields—a sad
commentary on the Dominican economy. It has often been said that
the academies exploit their young charges,[37] but this is an ethnocentric
argument that is only occasionally true and that overlooks a fundamental reality of Dominican life: the young man who signs with an academy
will receive a bonus and a first-year salary that together are roughly
seven times his father's annual income (assuming the father is not one
of the 30 percent of Dominicans who are unemployed). If the boy plays
for only four seasons (two years) he will outdistance all his friends at
home. For a time he will eat well, receive medical attention, and perhaps be a hero and a hope to all his less fortunate peers in sandlots and
ballfields throughout the Dominican Republic. Disappointing and frustrating his experience may be, but one cannot say that he will be exploited—not if one takes into account the current state of the Dominican Republic. He will have had a reprieve from the streets and from
unrewarding labor.

The dream of baseball shines radiantly for the individual, but it
blinds society. Baseball absorbs the energies of youth, energies better
spent in pursuit of other things. The dangers inherent in the dream of
escaping poverty through sport are manifest throughout the third world,
but they are especially so in the Dominican Republic because many
people know someone well who has succeeded in baseball. In a small
random sample that I surveyed around San Pedro de Macorís, ninety-
eight of a hundred respondents had a close friend or relative who had
signed a contract with an American club. The perception is that succeeding as a professional athlete is within everyone's reach; this is of
course an illusion, for there are not many job opportunities for Dominicans in baseball.

There are roughly forty-nine Dominicans in the major leagues, 325
in the minor leagues, and four hundred in Dominican baseball academies. Perhaps 250 play in the Dominican Professional League and are
unsigned by American clubs; another 250 are scouts, instructors, and
staff members affiliated with academies. Thus around thirteen hundred
Dominicans earn a living through professional baseball. The amount
of energy people expend in pursuit of a career in baseball appears
grotesquely out of proportion to the number of opportunities actually
available.

It can be argued, however, that Dominicans simply do not have other
options, and that this makes valid their investment in baseball. Edwards

counters this argument by saying that American blacks should focus on education rather than become involved in the "slave trade," as he refers to collegiate sport.[38] While educational opportunities for African-Americans in the United States are not as forthcoming as they are for whites, they are real and bountiful compared with what is available to the Dominicans. In my own view the impact of professional sport on individuals, which is salutary, must be distinguished from its impact on society, which has unfortunate consequences. What needs to be determined is the point at which the beneficial individual effects are outweighed by the detrimental societal effects. The socioeconomic conditions in the Dominican Republic are so distressing that one could argue that the point has already been reached: for all the success that the Dominicans have enjoyed at baseball, 80 percent of the people are unemployed or underemployed, and the economic benefits of baseball must be negligible. On the other hand there is no disputing the enormous success that some Dominican players have enjoyed. At least as far as baseball is concerned, it seems that the Dominicans' economic and political dependence on industrialized nations is both their best hope for the future and a leading cause of their underdevelopment.

And Dominican (and Latin American) dependence is growing. Perhaps the most distressing sign of this dependence is that the hallowed Caribbean Series has been transplanted to the United States.[39] This twelve-game round robin pits against one another the champions of the four winter leagues—those of Mexico, the Dominican Republic, Puerto Rico, and Venezuela—and in the past was held alternately in the four countries. The cost to the governments of sponsoring the series was not negligible, but it was borne because the series helped to build national pride. Now the sports promoter Rick Horrow (of the Senior Professional Baseball League) has agreed to pay the Caribbean Baseball Confederation $60,000 annually to hold the series, as well as all expenses (to be divided among the teams). From 1990 to 1992 it will be played at the Orange Bowl in Miami. When rumors first circulated in 1988 of the possible move to the United States, a reporter from the *New York Times* wrote that the economic benefits of such a shift were certain.[40] The president of the confederation, Horacio López-Díaz of Mexico, feared however that the series would lose its importance and following if it were held outside the Caribbean.

The opening of the series was disastrous. The Orange Bowl proved to be a poor facility for baseball, with a short left field fence and an uneven playing field. Officials from the host city did little to publicize or support the event, and the attendance for twelve games totaled only fifty thousand, despite the large Latino population in Miami. Cultural problems between Dominican fans and the local police almost led to a riot during one game. The affair was so disappointing that López swore the series would not be held in Miami when it was his country's turn to be the host.[41]

More recently there has been another sign of foreign domination of the game. A rumor is circulating that the North American baseball draft will soon include the Dominican Republic and Venezuela (it already includes Puerto Rico). This seems plausible in the light of the declining presence of African Americans in the game and the growing presence and importance of Latinos.

If the draft is extended to Dominican players, the immediate effect will be to drive up the cost of signing all players. (Puerto Rican players commonly sign for bonuses of $100,000, which is comparable to what other players get.) Another effect will be to diminish the power of the academies that are the principal threat to amateur baseball, and for this reason it may reinforce the control that the Dominicans have over the game. But at the same time a draft would allow North American interests to dictate further the structure of amateur baseball in the Dominican Republic.

But the logistical problems of implementing a draft in the Dominican Republic may outweigh the advantages of expanding the pool of available talent. The Puerto Rican draft is not strictly analogous, for in Puerto Rico ages and names can easily be verified, whereas in the Dominican Republic record keeping is far more haphazard.[42] It is also likely that teams with academies in the Dominican Republic would resist a draft because of the damage it would do to their position; teams with little or no presence in the country, on the other hand, would welcome it as an opportunity to sign players who would not otherwise be available to them.

I argue that all this further diminishes the autonomy and vitality of what was once a national sport. The best players are no longer playing at home or contributing much culturally to their less fortunate compatriots, and the game as a whole has been weakened. With the removal to the core countries of precious resources—talent and the Caribbean Series—neocolonialist underdevelopment is sure to continue.

4

The Wannabees

The Rookies at the
Academy, Their
Problems, and Avila

● ● ● ● ● ● ●

Nothing typifies the new direction of Dominican baseball as much as
the baseball academy, an institution rooted in the increased presence
and benevolent paternalism of North American baseball interests in the
country. In part the academies are a monument to Dominican success
in the sport, and in part they are a reaction to the problems that Dominicans have had in adjusting to life in American baseball. Campo Las
Palmas, the Dominican launching pad of the Los Angeles Dodgers, is
probably the best-run academy in the Dominican Republic, and its director, Ralph Avila, is a tireless, knowledgeable, and influential advo-
cate of the game.

In the mid-1970s only a few American major league teams had active
interests in the Dominican Republic: the Dodgers, the Pittsburgh Pirates, and the Toronto Blue Jays. Most teams were content to establish a
minimal working relationship with the Dominican clubs and to assign a
scout who would cover the Dominican Republic along with the rest of
the Caribbean. In 1972 the Dodgers assigned to the Dominican Republic one of their better scouts, Ralph Avila. When the Blue Jays became more interested in developing Dominican talent they hired Epy
Guerrero, a Dominican who had been a failed player in the American
minor league system. Like so many good baseball men, Guerrero had
an ability to spot talent and develop ballplayers that far outweighed his
shortcomings as a player.

Guerrero and Avila soon became the most productive scouts and developers of talent in Dominican baseball. In the mid-1970s they roamed the country and signed talent wherever they spotted it; they were joined by a few others, such as Howie Haak of the Pittsburgh Pirates. As the Dominican Republic became known as the place to sign excellent and abundant talent cheaply, the competition between scouts escalated considerably. Until 1984 there were no restrictions on the way scouts operated in the country, and most simply signed as many players as their budgets allowed. Concern for the development of prospects beyond getting their signature on paper was uneven, depending on the good will of the scout. The reasoning at the time was that the ballplayers would make it or break it in the American rookie leagues: "Before [the academies] a lot of players were signed in this country, taken to the U.S. and released—nine, ten, maybe more in one day—because the kids weren't ready. That wasn't fair." [1]

Guerrero and Avila both were eager to sign the best players but differed in how much responsibility they felt toward them. Guerrero strove primarily to secure the talent: "Well, I think it's my job to sign the players. [The Toronto Blue Jays organization] should be the ones to handle the players after they're signed." [2] Much more was at stake for Avila: "I say we had only five or six problems in all the thousands we've looked at. But, the rest of the Latinos is another story. Somebody once said to me, 'We're not looking for boy scouts.' I say, 'But we're looking for decent people.' These boys got enough problems in the United States." [3]

Avila feels that getting a young Dominican interested in baseball is getting a finger in the dike, helping to prevent him from turning to drugs and a life of crime. He knows his milieu well. He is as interested in having boys develop into "decent people" as he is in signing them, even if he must occasionally lose one: "When scouts sign a ballplayer they mention only the easy, good things. When I sign a ballplayer I say the opposite . . . I say this is the toughest job in the world. It'll be easier to go to the sugar cane field and be choppin' cane ten hours a day. Now baseball is a job. In this factory you're gonna work twenty-four hours a day. Now you gonna know the truth, you wanna sign? I had only one person who was honest enough to say that it wasn't for him . . . I shook his hand and walked away. I was glad for him." [4]

Although Avila has a sense of morality about his work, he is not easily taken advantage of, nor does his morality cloud his judgment of talent or his ability to succeed against the competition. On the contrary, when I asked Avila how he could get along with Toronto's superscout Guerrero, who has a legendary reputation for stealing ballplayers, he replied: "We have a saying, 'Dog don't eat dog.'" Avila knows what it takes to gain the inside track on a prospect. He will help out the player's family, perhaps getting someone a job or a loan. One of Avila's competitors steals many ballplayers by telling their mothers how well their sons will be cared for. These are the more effective scouts. Most others are barely concerned with building trust and accountability.

Avila envisioned a baseball academy as early as 1974, even though Guerrero eventually got his own academy off the ground earlier than Avila did (in 1977). When he first moved to the Dominican Republic Avila advised his friend Monchín Pichardo, president of the Licey Tigers, to cut costs by curbing the enormous number of players he kept as reserves. Avila reasoned that with the money saved Pichardo could either pay his regular players more or open a baseball school where prospects could try out. If the prospects looked good they could be kept with the team and paid until they were ready to play in the United States.

Pichardo was so smitten with the idea that he decided to begin the academy on his own and asked Avila to direct it. After Avila secured permission to do this from Al Campanis, vice president of the Dodgers, he set about developing members of Licey for Pichardo. The academy the two men fashioned was intended exclusively for the Licey club and included professional players from a number of American major league franchises, which eventually so dissatisfied Avila that he pressed the Dodgers for his own academy. Avila recalled to me how the long road that he took culminated in the best baseball complex in the country: "In the [Licey] academy we had eleven players from the Dodgers organization, and seventy from different teams because all the scouts, when they sign a player, wanna give them to Monchín because he takes better care of players. Licey is one of the most popular clubs here. We had only 11 players that belong to the Dodgers, though."[5]

By 1981 Avila decided to break away from the Licey academy and form his own. Guerrero had by then already set a successful precedent. With the help of his assistant Elvio Jiménez, a former major leaguer, Avila left for San Pedro de Macorís. He persuaded Pichardo to continue subsidizing his small group of Licey players (many of whom were Dodger prospects) and began what was the precursor to Campo Las Palmas:

> We had a boarding house . . . We started with twelve ballplayers, and we started to hire unsigned amateurs to the academy: work with them, develop their skills. Now at that time we only had a house because we don't have much of a budget. We built two rooms in Elvio's backyard and we put eight beds in each room, and Elvio's wife fed them. If she spent $150 on food, we'd pay her back. Now, we get results. We sent better conditioned ballplayers to the U.S., players with better knowledge: Peña, Reyes,

Duncan. We made a proposal to Peter [O'Malley, president of the Dodgers], and he realized that it was worth the investment to build a complex. By that time Toronto was ahead of us. They had an academy and a big budget.[6]

The Dodgers continued to move slowly, deciding at first to fund the San Pedro Academy rather than build their own complex. In the meantime the annual budget of the Blue Jays' academy had reached $100,000, and the Philadelphia Phillies also were beginning to invest heavily in the Dominican Republic. In 1984 the Dodgers finally gave Avila their approval for the complex. Even then Avila and Campanis were faced with the interesting problem of convincing O'Malley of how best to accomplish the task "Dominican style": they were trying to do the job cost-effectively, as they had been asked to do, but O'Malley suddenly changed his ideas when he became enamored with a particular piece of property:

> We were riding around with one of Peter [O'Malley]'s friends, and he asked us, "You wanna see my farm? It's only ten kilometers from here." He had a sugar cane farm, and we took the road to Guerra. When we got [to where the academy is now] we saw the "For Sale" sign on the property across the street. We looked at the property for sale, and Peter said, "I don't like this place at all, but that one over there [pointing to our place], I like." It was a hill! There were cows and horses all over the place. It looked like a jungle . . . If you realize that we spent approximately $400,000 for the land, the construction of the entire camp, baseball fields, leveling the hill, equipment, the bus, you see how far the money goes, and what a good deal it was for the Dodgers. Imagine what this would cost in the United States![7]

The Setting

The finished complex looks more like one of the posh resorts along the coast than the sugar cane plantations around it. The fifty acres of Campo Las Palmas are beautifully manicured, with two fields (a third is being added), modern buildings, and the most modern equipment. All is new, well maintained, and clean. At this plush academy the rookies are ministered to and instructed. They take daily practice and play two seasons a year: winter (November to February) and summer (June to September).

One of the boys told me that all the rookies at other camps envy the those at Camp Las Palmas because they look so professional and travel in a team bus that bears a highly visible Dodger logo. Those who run Campo Las Palmas aim to instill pride and professionalism in the wannabees—those who want to be ballplayers. When the Dodger rookies play they are dressed in Dodger uniforms that are well cared for, never dirty or disheveled. It is the proudest and most physically disciplined of the rookie clubs.

It is common for rookies at Campo Las Palmas never to have slept in a bed that has sheets. The dormitory is immaculate, and all Dodger rookies are taught to care for their beds as much as for their equipment. They also learn other basic skills: how to act in a group (in a weight room or television room, for example), how to keep a place clean. Those who cannot learn are released, but most sense that they are part of something special and are up to the challenge.

Two diamonds on either side of the building complex anchor the camp. One has the dimensions and characteristics of a major league park; the other is for practice only. A raised concrete walkway shaded by a permanent awning interconnects the dormitories, locker rooms, dining room, amusement center, and other facilities. Behind the baseball diamonds and concealed by the dense growth around Campo Las Palmas is a working farm, with sugar cane, pulp, yucca, and chickens. This farm partly subsidizes the academy by providing the rookies with food valued at around ten thousand pesos a year. Avila is assisted by a staff that includes six instructors and scouts, groundskeepers and maintenance service, and secretarial help.

A major league franchise that sends its best coaches and instructors to a particular country clearly has confidence in the talent that it sees there, and its investment in the country in turn makes the caliber of play higher. The Los Angeles Dodgers cut no corners. They regularly send excellent instructors to the Dominican Republic. Leading pitching and batting coaches were there during one of my stays in December 1987. Another time, in January 1989, a batting instructor was flown to Campo Las Palmas to consult with the staff and teach his techniques to the rookies. The staff at the better Dominican academies is steeped in baseball. All the instructors and scouts at Campo Las Palmas have played baseball in the United States, some in the major leagues. Avila has managed and taught the game at almost every level for four decades.

Signing a Wannabee

In the past signing players was really the only business of the American baseball scouts in the Dominican Republic: they would sign a prospect and ship him to the United States to see if he could climb the baseball

ladder. With the era of the academies the entire process of readying a
prospect became longer and more complicated. Signing the prospect is
now only the beginning.

Whether a young hopeful comes to the academy for a tryout on his
own initiative or at the invitation of a scout, the experience is nerve-
wracking and sometimes traumatic. I often watched prospects come to
Campo Las Palmas, their hopes and fears etched on their faces:

> The story is different in the dusty faces of these young ballplay-
> ers. The pitcher on the mound kicks high, revealing underwear
> through the torn baseball pants, his hat partially split on the side,
> and spikes with too many years on them. He releases his best fast
> ball and barely controls it.
>
> Ralph walks up to him. It's a slow motion walk, and the fear
> has time to well up in the pitcher all over again. Is he gone?
> Ralph doesn't say a word, takes hold of the kid's pitching hand
> turning it over palm up, and begins kneading it looking for cal-
> louses. The kid looks bewildered. Ralph lets the moment sink in,
> telling him finally that he's releasing the ball incorrectly and
> showing him how to throw it right.
>
> The Tryout goes back to throwing and within two or three
> pitches the boy is throwing incorrectly again. He knows it, too,
> but the poor kid is so nervous he can't control himself. Avila and
> the others stand behind him commenting on all sorts of things.
> Some chuckle, some hem and haw. The kid is straining and you
> can see it in his pitches as he aims and overstrides on each pitch.
> He looks back at Avila and the others furtively, and only after a
> pause that must have seemed interminable, do they decide to
> bring him in for a thirty-day trial.[8]

This young player is in the door.

The Dodger staff has the tryouts down to a routine: they look for the
tools (speed, arm strength, hitting ability), observe the player's body
type, try to determine his aptitude. Their talk is about "bat speed," "me-
chanics," and bodily dimensions. The axe falls swiftly if a player does
not have at least the basics. The staff members care, but so many prospects come to their gates that they have to be a bit distant, perhaps to
protect themselves. Avila says, "This is still, after all these years, the
hardest part of the job." The wannabees seek desperately to overcome
their distance from the scouts and take neither failure nor discouragement as final. One rookie illustrated the determination of the young
tryout as he reflected on his initial failure to impress the Dodgers: "Eleo-
doro asked me when I could come to San Pedro so they could look at
me. That day my speed [pitchers are clocked on a radar gun for velocity]

was 74–75. They told me I couldn't stay in the [dorms] in San Pedro because I didn't have the necessary speed. So I went back home, and spent two months practicing. So the next time they sent for me my speed was 78–79. Avila gave the authorization for my stay."[9]

As for the successful prospect, he has not been signed, and he will not be until he has been screened more thoroughly. This is one thing the academy has accomplished: it has made all prospects subject to intense scrutiny in a variety of situations.

The boy who has passed the first hurdle will be living alongside the regular rookies and practicing with them, but because he has not been signed he is not eligible to play; he is not a professional. His parents will be asked to sign an agreement that outlines the responsibilities of the team toward their son. The boy will have insurance and medical coverage only during the month that he is at the academy. Sometimes parents have to be told repeatedly that their son has not signed a professional contract. As a "tryout" the boy will not be allowed to wear the regular Dodger uniform; instead he will have a jersey like those worn in batting practice. Although the prospects do not mind being clothed differently, they are visually set off from the other players and required to prove themselves in ways that the others are not. They have to show quick improvement and the capacity to learn, to be coachable:

> In that period of thirty days he stays with us. If somebody makes him an offer, he can go and sign with another organization. Normally, we make the evaluation in the first week. We scout for tools, not for performance . . . There are five tools, and if you got 'em, we can teach you. Hitting, nobody knows, but if you got power, you're gonna show it as soon as you make contact. In one week, we get the faculty to evaluate you. When you run the hundred-yard dash in our camp, it's on a good track; and if you don't have the proper shoes, we loan them to you.
>
> The rest of the month, they're gonna show us their habits: their drive, dedication, determination, desire, durability. [The] five D's. If they got the tools, then we keep them.[10]

Signing a young player is straightforward. By the end of the trial period the staff will have discussed this possibility with the player's parents. The player himself will have become comfortable with the idea of being a Dodger wannabee, having shown ability, desire, and emotional strength. In addition to his signing bonus (which averages $4,000 with the Dodgers) he will earn $700 for each of the six months that he plays, as well as room and board.

This is a tremendous sum for anyone in the Dominican Republic,

and the academy has had difficulty teaching the prospects how to manage their money. The subject is sometimes given short shrift because
there are so many others: baseball, hygiene, English, social skills. One
can expect a certain amount of extravagance from young men who have
never before had so much money. Some rookies quickly buy expensive
radios ("boom boxes") that they carry everywhere, and others spend
their money wildly on gold chains. One wannabee went down the
streets of San Pedro de Macorís handing out twenty-peso notes to anyone he met. But many rookies buy staples for their brothers and sisters
or just turn turn the money over to their families, who put in new roofs,
do repairs, or make hospital appointments that have been long delayed.

The Dodger Wannabees

The academy has three tiers of players: tryouts, prospective rookies, and
rookies. The makeup of the academy changes constantly as people are
moved up or weeded out. This makes it difficult, though not impossible, to generalize about life in Campo Las Palmas.

The typical Dodger cohort comprises between thirty and forty players, who may be in residence for as long as two years. Despite the preva-
lence of poor boys at the academy, a fair number of rookies are the
middle-class sons of journalists, clerks, and teachers. In the cohort that
I followed in 1987–89, six of thirty boys were high school graduates.
This is a relatively high proportion for the Dominican Republic, perhaps because the prominence of Campo Las Palmas enables the Dodgers
to be more selective than other teams. Class differences are not often
consciously expressed at Campo Las Palmas, and when they are, then
usually in terms of education. A young high school graduate who attended the camp recalled: "Sometimes, one can feel ashamed of certain
guys because they have a low educational background. I don't blame
them because they have enough education to behave correctly, but
many times I try to keep my distance from certain boys." [11]

The popular belief that all Dominican baseball players come from
San Pedro de Macorís is not borne out at Campo Las Palmas. The rookies come from all over the country, from other parts of the Caribbean
and Latin America (during my stay at the academy two Venezuelans
and a Puerto Rican were there), from big cities like Santo Domingo and
from small hamlets. Their varied origins show to what lengths the
scouts will go in their search for talent.

Throughout the Caribbean one finds social distinctions made along
racial lines. The intersections of race and class form a labyrinth of be-

havior and attitudes. Race relations in the Dominican Republic bear some similarities to those of North America, but there are strong differences as well. Because 75 percent of all Dominicans are mulatto (another 10 percent are black), there is no such thing as racial purity: racial differences are relative rather than absolute. In general the more Hispanic a person is, the higher and "whiter" the person's class and social position will be; the more racially African a person is, the lower these will be. Dominicans and other Caribbean peoples equate race with social class, and race consciousness is high. But there is nowhere near the animosity about race that one finds in North America; the prevailing attitude could be described with cruel irony as racism without malice. I recall a telling example: in class one day some of the darker boys insisted on touching my hair (it is light brown and very fine), which they called "hair that moves in the wind." To them my hair was clearly a superordinate class trait, but at the same time they marveled at it and were not hesitant about touching it.

Social status in the academy is often likely to be viewed in terms of race. On several occasions the boys would make comments about the race of someone who was darker or lighter. At times this was met with resigned acceptance, at other times with disapproval both from the person at whom the comments were directed and from other boys. One afternoon in English class I was going over a dialogue with two boys, one darker than the other. In the middle of the dialogue, and for no apparent reason, the lighter-skinned boy unscrewed his ballpoint pen and showed me the ink refill. He then smiled, pointed to the blue-black ink, and nodded in the direction of his darker colleague. The dark-skinned boy smiled weakly, acquiescing in a form of racism that he had obviously endured many times.

At other times jokes made in English class about race angered the darker-skinned boys. (While I heard darker rookies joke about their own darkness, I never heard a darker-skinned boy make a racial joke about a lighter-skinned colleague.) What underlies much racial humor in the Dominican Republic is the suggestion that the butt of the joke is Haitian—a nationality that is widely disdained in the Dominican Republic. To see if race was a factor in social clustering I observed the boys on the team bus, in the dining room, in the dugout, and in the classroom, and saw little of what could be termed racial segregation. Only their socializing at home seemed to follow a racial pattern (although a lack of complete data for everyone at the academy leaves this question open), for even when a boy had both darker and lighter friends at the academy, at home he tended to socialize with those who lived in his neighborhood or town. These friends were often from the same class and of the same color. In general, however, racial harmony seems to be the rule at Campo Las Palmas.

The wannabees at Campo Las Palmas learn to treat social and economic differences as mere personal distinctions. The program of discipline and cadre of strict instructors bridge these schisms and make the Dodger rookies focus their efforts and energies on beating the other rookie teams rather than on antagonizing each other. The structure of the academy is ideally suited to displacing competition and aggression outside the group.

Avila runs the camp as a modified military school. He has very pronounced ideas about the role of discipline and routine in the conditioning of young athletes. (It is important to bear in mind that Latino culture is somewhat more inclined toward authoritarian relations than white, liberal, middle-class America is.) Avila will brook no disrespect: the guiding principles of the academy are respect for oneself and respect for others, and particularly respect for authority.

Initially I found somewhat authoritarian the heavy emphasis on regimentation at Campo Las Palmas, but as I became more familiar with the young prospects I gained respect for Avila's training strategy. Because of their backgrounds most of the boys needed discipline; many were brought up in poor homes and spent much of their life unsupervised, in the streets and away from home. With only two exceptions these were not boys who were bad or rejected by their parents; they were simply from large families with many siblings and parents who worked long hours. At the other end of the socioeconomic spectrum in the academy were the sons of middle-class families. These boys tended to have been overindulged, particularly if there had been daughters in the house. Like the poorer boys they could be undisciplined, preoccupied, coddled, and spoiled (as talented athletes can sometimes be). Whether these traits were the result of their upbringing or rather their abundance of talent and the way people responded to it, Avila knew they were counterproductive.

The rookies often thought of playing in the United States only in terms of the money it offered them. Avila knew that there was more to it than this, that life in the American major leagues was difficult in ways the boys could not imagine. If they flourished or even if they only survived it would be because they were disciplined, determined, and prepared: "You gotta be thinking about baseball all the time. You travel in buses with no air conditioning, sleep in [lousy] hotels, eat strange foods with people who you can't talk with. You have a manager, and you don't know if he [don't] like you as a Negro, or he don't like you as a Latino. You don't know who you're gonna be facing. The four or five years you spend in the minors you're gonna be suffering. Only 3 per cent of the ballplayers we sign make it to the big leagues. The other 97 percent fail and have to come back here and go to work in a factory or sugar cane fields."[12]

The Academy as Socializing Agent

What the academy does in the time spent with the rookies goes far beyond teaching baseball skills to talented young men. At various points career preparation gives way to socialization, as the rookies learn how to move up the organizational ladder and how to cope with the cultural changes they will face in North America. For many the stay at the academy coincides roughly with the transition from adolescence to adulthood.

The Dodgers have studied this problem for a long time (when Campanis was a vice president with the team he and Avila had eighty years of experience between them), and the team has concluded that many of the problems are the result of the slower physical and emotional development of many of these impoverished prospects: "On the average, the Latin players are signed at a critical age when they are evolving from adolescence to manhood. These adjustments have to be made without the help of their parents, in a strange country [the United States], where they are not familiar with the environment, and where the language, food, and customs are different . . . Most come from poor families who live in villages, sugar cane fields and have never seen the average American city. Most have never held a paying job, and know little about earning and spending money."[13]

Many if not most of the academies have little concern for the comprehensive development of their players. A few, however, believe that their charge includes preparing the young men for a range of social and psychological transitions. Perhaps they are not always motivated by social responsibility, but rather by the desire to diminish the chances that they will lose their prospects as they make their way through the minor leagues. The socialization of this age-graded set of men bears a certain resemblance to male initiation rites studied by anthropologists around the world.[14] Ritualized gender bonding, isolation from the general population, massive amounts of instruction, and anxiety over the changes to come all mark the processes Van Gennep termed the "rites of passage,"[15] the culmination of which is the social and psychological transformation of the young novice. In this regard Campo Las Palmas is a sort of Dominican finishing school, and its rituals may be likened to the initiation rites of the East African pastoralists, the Katchina ceremonials of the Pueblos of the Southwest, or the boot camps of the U.S. Marines.

But the baseball academy is different in that it follows a stricter system of merit: only some initiates pass on to the next level, and because the threat of failure is more real than in other initiation systems, it causes that much more anxiety. A well-run academy can channel this anxiety constructively and use it to strengthen the players' effort and determination. Often this is not difficult because of the large rewards that accrue to the players who make it to the majors leagues.

Changes in Perception and Reality

If a rookie is to move successfully through the academy he must be willing to change, and the organization must be capable of making him change. Both player and organization are negotiating their expectations (their goals) and their behavior. Both stand to benefit from the success of their endeavor, although the player stands to benefit much more.

The young rookie need not be told that his arrival at the academy is the most important thing in his life, for he may well be his family's only hope for escaping poverty. One rookie made a typical comment when he was asked whether he was anxious on his arrival at the academy: "I felt very nervous, very emotional, because many young men want to be here, and only we had the opportunity to work here, and to try to fulfill our dreams of becoming big league players."[16]

The eagerness and need of the rookies breed high expectations, often excessively so. When reality falls short of these expectations many problems result—some peculiar to one player and others to one club, and still others generally characteristic of Latinos. It is important to distinguish these categories from one another if a club is to have an effective policy toward Latino players. The Dodgers have implicitly understood this and have made good use of their academy to transform the rookies into effective players and help them make cultural adjustments.

Many things change the way the novices perceive themselves, including the need to follow a rigidly structured daily regimen. A typical day looks like this:

7:00 A.M. to 8:30 A.M.	Breakfast
9:30 to 10:00	All players dressed in uniform of the day
10:00 to 10:30	Clubhouse meeting
10:30 to 11:00	Stretching and running
11:00 to 11:30	Warming up and pepper
11:30 to 12:30 P.M.	Cappers (double play drill)
12:30 to 1:30	Lunch

1:30 to 2:30	Infield practice and pitchers practice covering first base
2:30 to 3:30	Tossing and batting practice, machines in cages
3:30 to 4:00	Running the bases and cool-down exercises
4:00 to 5:00	Showers
5:00 to 6:00	English class ($5.00 penalty for missed class)
6:00 to 7:30	Dinner
7:30 to 10:30	Free time
10:30	Curfew: Players must be in bed
11:00	Lights and radios must be off

On days when there is a game the schedule is adjusted to allow for travel (for away games) or preparation (for games at Campo Las Palmas). If they must travel the players are dressed and on the bus by 9:00 A.M.. The game generally begins at 10:30 or 11:00 and lasts until roughly 1:00 P.M.. Then the players return to the camp for a late lunch and various forms of training until they have their English class.

This schedule leaves the players less time to get in trouble or to get bored. Avila has the boys perform other duties, some having to do with hygiene, others with the care of clothing and equipment. As in any other socialization program, the chores are aimed at instilling responsibility in the boys. Not only will self-discipline make each ballplayer more likely to succeed at baseball, but it will redound to the benefit of his teammates.

The league structure of the academies and the games played between them make for bonding among teammates. The rookies are initiates into the world of professional baseball, and like initiates everywhere they find that their egos must be subordinated to the interests of the group if the individual members are to succeed. But even while the members of a team learn to bond, they undergo profound social and psychological changes in a highly structured environment. Unlike their counterparts in North America, the Dominican rookies must prepare for cultural changes in addition to preparing for a career.

Changes in Self-Perception

If the rookies at Campo Las Palmas chafe at the behavioral and attitudinal changes demanded of them, they nevertheless acquiesce because they realize how much hinges on their doing so; the authoritarian presence of Avila helps ensure this as well. Gradually the rookie learns not only to play better baseball but to follow a routine that begins when he wakes up, continues as he eats and studies, and ends only when he goes to bed.

Carefully built and carefully maintained, the Dodger academy is intended to overwhelm both visitor and rookie. The message is that those in the Dodger organization are better simply because they are Dodgers; the effect of the message is to make the young wannabees open to change. The Dodger rookies are known throughout the league for their crisp, laundered uniforms (different ones for games at home and games on the road). Everything from the Dodger logo on the team bus to the visits by famous players to the academy makes the rookies feel that they will transcend the limits of the academy. Every season one hears them making optimistic claims that this is the year they will get to play in the United States.

Teaching Dodger Ball

The summer rookie league consists of seventy-two games, the winter league of sixty. Like their parent clubs the rookie teams have games home and away, team uniforms, a team bus. A player who only months before may have seen the rookie league as forbiddingly professional soon becomes accustomed to it, and playing baseball becomes as automatic as walking. The difference is that now he is wearing the uniform of a professional and has a crew of instructors yelling at him to keep his head down and his eyes on the ball. The life of a rookie is much the same in the United States, but in the Dominican Republic these exhortations are given round the clock. Teaching a young prospect is only one of Avila's jobs. He must first unteach him, rid him of lifelong habits. To accomplish this he resorts to endless repetition. Each play must be a reflex, a product of what Avila calls "muscle memory."

Coaching and coachability are what the rookie leagues are all about. Instruction cannot succeed without them. There were at least six prospects in the academy during my work there who possessed all the tools but were not taking to the instruction. Some players resist changing ways that have served them. Others simply lack intelligence. I was once asked by Avila what I thought of a certain player out on the field, and I remarked that I thought he had more natural ability than most of the others. Avila agreed but said the prospect was not smart enough to realize his physical potential. I had to concur, based only on the player's work in the English class I helped manage. Prospects like this pose special, frustrating problems for the staff. The instructors can improve a player's muscle memory, but they cannot increase his intelligence. Still other prospects have attitudes that make them difficult to coach. This is perhaps the worst kind of player to instruct: one with skills and intelligence, but no understanding that he has anything more to learn. Some prospects of this kind go on to the major leagues simply because they have so much talent, but many others fail:

> I had one kid at Vero Beach [the Dodgers' spring training facility]. He was a Puerto Rican kid. That kid had some tools! I signed him when he was playing in an international tournament of nine countries, and he was only sixteen years old. We saw him and said, "He's the next Clemente." He was the youngest on the team, batting fourth in the lineup. He had an arm, strength, good power, good outfielder. He can play third base and catcher too. A scout's dream! As good as he was, he was that stupid. Not in intelligence. He just didn't think he needed to work hard. We protected him on a major league roster; and with all the tools he had, he landed in Mexico. He just had bad habits, not off the field, but on it. Wouldn't listen to anybody.[17]

There are also stories of men who made it to the major leagues and succeeded, only to become "head cases": they would no longer listen to advice and often achieved far less than their potential.

At the academy players who are apt to become head cases can be spotted and their problems can sometimes be averted (see the discussion below). Campo Las Palmas operates on principles of discipline and routine, partly because the young players have never had it, and partly because they will soon be immersed in a new culture. The primary rule is to respect authority; there are also many little, seemingly insignificant things that young men are expected to do. Sometimes the discipline gets striking results. One young man who signed in fall 1987 had all the tools but was a bully—aggressive, belligerent, and surly toward his fellow players and everyone else. Once he refused to put his dirty laundry into the piles set aside for this purpose, which led to a confrontation with the laundress and eventually his ejection from the laundry room. But within the month he was a changed man: he publicly apologized to everyone in the camp and never tormented people again.

Problems Facing the Dodger Wannabees

Most young men are highly unlikely to get to the major leagues. The road to the majors is arduous, and more so for the Latino player. The smallest thing becomes a problem. Communication problems head the list, but there are others just as pressing, and they begin at the academy.

It is not always possible to keep the boys out of trouble without their

getting bored. One reason Campo Las Palmas is outside Santo Domingo is to isolate the players from the various diversions of city life, but
this can lead to boredom and boredom leads to arguments. Boredom is
what prospects at the camp complain about the most. Even though
most of their waking hours are filled with activities, they still have
ample time to lounge about during parts of the weekdays and all of the
weekends. For a time the boys could spend their free hours in the
nearby town of Guerra. But the boys, aged seventeen to twenty-one,
were irresistibly and understandably drawn to the young women in
town, who in turn saw the chance of becoming involved with a future
Dodger (and perhaps marrying him) as a way of escaping from their
backwoods existence. A few scrapes in Guerra ensued, in what seemed
like a Dominican counterpart to the "town and gown" problems that
plague American universities, and the staff at the academy declared
Guerra off limits. Most of the young men now head for home on the
weekends, and some do so each day. The few who stay at the academy
on weekends endure the worst kind of boredom, one that often leads to
disputes over the most insignificant issues: I once saw some boys argue
about which cartoons (*muñequitos*) to watch on television.

Conflict through Competition, Temperament, and Lifestyle

One of my main interests in studying the academy as a socializing agent
was to see what tensions existed between the Dominican values held by
the rookies and the North American values imparted through baseball. I
was interested in particular in how Dominican notions of cooperation
might conflict with the competitive values inherent in the North American style of play and reinforced by the academy. An interesting kind of
social tension arises from competition, and I assumed that it would
cause increased competition and jealousy (*envidia*) among the boys at
the academy. But when I asked the players whether the scarcity of major
league jobs in the United States caused competitive tensions, I got a
mixed response. It was difficult to know when to ascribe tension to
competition and when to ascribe it to other causes. No clear pattern
emerged, although I sought to narrow my inquiry by looking specifi-
cally at players competing for the same position, and by asking players
how they felt when others got to the United States before they did:

> Most guys feel that they hope the other guys make it. I don't
> think they get jealous too much, because each one feels that he
> could sign up with another club [if he doesn't make it at this
> academy].[18]

I didn't feel too well [about other guys going to the States]. I felt happy for them, but I thought that I had done good defensive work and I deserved to go too. I felt bad the first days, but this year I do my job to see if I can travel next year.[19]

Yes, Alan, there is some jealousy. Among us pitchers there sometimes is. We argue a lot because sometimes one of the boys is feeling superior to others.[20] But the majority get along well.[21]

Leveling Inequalities

Egalitarian societies have means of combating social inequalities.[22] The ability of the group to go about its business depends on it. These means are much in evidence at Campo Las Palmas.

One example is the tendency of older, more experienced players to look after the newer recruits, who are made anxious by their new surroundings and by having to leave behind all they know; this makes for a more coherent group both on and off the field. Another is the thirty-day tryout period, which enables the new arrivals to become familiar with the camp and its culture:

> The guys who have been here, like me for instance, we help the new guys. I'm a shortstop working with that new guy over there from Puerto Plata.[23]

> Once [the new arrivals] sign, they are taken on. As long as they [don't have a] swelled head we get along.[24]

> Well, I felt strange with the kids [at the camp], but I already got to know them better. They were nice to me because last year another Venezuelan guy had been here.[25]

> I was a little nervous [during my first days at the camp], but I already knew Eleodoro, and he told me how things were.[26]

On occasion, however, a new arrival will be overly defensive, and this is manifested in a belligerence toward others. Or he may feel superior to others, and the group will have to "level" him. This is part of the process of internal socialization that goes on within the cohort, and may include ostracism, ridicule, or verbal confrontation: "The new [arrivals] are taught by those who have been here. Like, I help that new guy, the second baseman over there. If they have an attitude—well, that's a different story. We turn our backs on them, the hot dogs. We have a new guy, D——, and he is that way. Last week we played and the umps called him out twice sliding into second. Afterward the ump explained that he thought it was close, but that the guy was a jerk, so he called him out. We all agreed and laughed. He needs it."[27]

On recalling his entry into the group, another rookie admitted to having been "a little crazy" when he initially bullied some of the others. One by one the members of the group ignored him, until in his loneliness he accommodated himself to them; arguments over which television shows to watch gave way to the sharing of jokes. Often a sense of racial or class inferiority lies beneath the belligerence. As the new arrival feels less threatened, the group is more generous and the barriers recede.

Many members of the group are sensitive to the troublemaker. One rookie articulated the views held by the whole group as he addressed the issue of defensive behavior in terms of class and education: "Sometimes one feels ashamed of certain guys because they have a low educational background. I don't blame them because they don't have enough education, but that's why I try to keep my distance from certain guys. I'd rather hang around with the people that can teach me good things."[28]

Some members of the group enjoy a particularly high status because of their baseball skills or the likelihood that they will succeed, and they sometimes use their position to correct unpleasant situations or restore stability. One well-respected rookie described what he did when two new arrivals got into a fight in their dormitory: "These kinds of things happen between us sometimes, and when [the new arrivals] do something I think is wrong, I tell them. Some of them do this fake boxing with each other. Sometimes these games can turn into real fights. I don't approve of that, and stop it."[29] Another senior rookie recalled: "It happens with the boys that have been signed lately that they try to show they're superior, and I'm not that kind of player. They try to show they're real machos. They try to show they're more elegant in the field. I tell them, it's not elegance that makes a good player. You can't be a good player with your mouth; you have to show them you have [guts]."[30]

While the group tends to level out inequalities, there are nevertheless daily tensions and conflicts that result from living together:

> Some kids borrow clothes and I don't like it when other people wear my personal things. And sometimes they don't even return to you what they borrowed from you.[31]

> Well, you see in all groups there are guys who are troublemakers. I don't want to say their names. I don't like them because they try to make trouble: they try to be the best [show off], they try to drink sometimes when they are in training. Then they come back in the morning and talk about it. I don't like that.[32]

I do not wish to imply that the atmosphere at Las Palmas is one of unrelieved conflict: the young men there are more caring than competitive. Whatever doubts I may have had were dispelled when I saw the boys bid farewell to each other as the more fortunate left the academy for the United States. There were no signs of resentment: a number of boys wept openly, others spoke proudly of their fellows who were enjoying good seasons in the United States. These comments by two of the boys put all the social problems of the camp in perspective:

> I like it here [at Campo Las Palmas]. It's quiet and we share time with the mates. We talk about our little troubles with our friends here. [33]

> [The other boys from the academy] sometimes go to my house by the sea. And we have spent some time together away from here. Here, we watch TV, eat sugar cane, and talk about our future. We have a good time together. [34]

Problems in the Promised Land

The cultural alienation the boys face when they reach the United States inevitably leads some of them to abandon their quest for achieving fame through baseball. It is fairly common for a player to return to the Dominican Republic, to a town and a people more familiar and accepting. More often, though, he becomes ensnared in self-destructive behavior off the field, particularly problematic relationships with women and drugs. Figures are difficult to gather; most of my information comes from statements by people who are very familiar with the problem, and from cases I know of firsthand or have read about. The director of scouting for one American League team pointedly told me that all the problems he had had in his organization that year had been caused by Dominicans. The head of a Dominican baseball association cited the lack of education of many Dominican players as a factor: "It's a shame that [adjustment problems in the United States] had to happen to Dominican players. To Americans it doesn't happen as much. Different background. The background of Dominican players is different. Most of the ballplayers from the States, they graduate high school. Over here, they rarely get through sixth grade. Another thing is the experience of going from a poor situation to having it all. It's something very hard to get used to." [35] Whether or not their problems of adjustment are a direct result of poor education, Dominican novices can expect to have them. These problems can however be alleviated if the player is prepared for them and has the right temperament. It is important to distinguish aggravation over unimportant slights from frustration over real problems with the player and the organization.

Culture, food, American colleagues, and American fans all have the potential to cause problems, but language is perhaps the greatest problem of all. One reason is that when they are in the Dominican Republic the players tend to underestimate the value of learning English. After a particularly grueling English session in his baseball academy, one talented prospect said to me (in Spanish), "Jorge Bell, forty-seven home runs, two million dollars, and he doesn't speak English." (He was right on the first two counts, wrong on the third.) But this casual attitude changes once a player gets to the United States. Virtually everyone I spoke to who had recently played there mentioned the language barrier as frightening and formidable:

> We didn't know the English language. We used to go to McDonald's, but we couldn't order anything because we didn't speak English.[36]

> We didn't talk to anybody. We just saw and touched things and handed people money. With the food, we ate chicken and turkey all the time.[37]

Dominicans who played in the United States thirty and forty years ago also mentioned language difficulties as paramount. One former major leaguer recalled: "We had a lotta problems then. Now its easy for them because we got schools to teach them English. But when I went I didn't know English, I couldn't order in a restaurant, even simple things. I didn't know the kind of lives you live in the United States. It was kinda hard for us to make it. Lots of guys, they didn't make it. They came back because they couldn't adjust."[38]

A Dominican player may be fortunate enough to room with a Latino teammate when he first joins an American team, but this does not always make his transition easier. It may lessen the culture shock that the player experiences, but it can also lead him to rely excessively on others and interfere with his learning of English, as it did with one player: "I didn't know what to expect. I spoke two or three words of English. I was lucky. I had with me the whole time a New York Rican [a Puerto Rican living in New York]. He was with the Yankees, I think he's in jail now. We used to go together. Anything I need to do they could help me to do it. Translate. I never was able to speak. I don't think I could have managed [without them]."[39] Another player modestly attributes his better grasp of English to having been forced to learn it: "I don't know what happened to me with English. Mine is a really broken English, but I learned it because I had three Americans as roomies."[40]

The language barrier has greater implications for some kinds of players than for others. Certain positions, such as catcher and pitcher, absolutely require language competency. The director of one academy recalled that he had two talented catchers and could not advance either because of the language problems they were unable to overcome: "I got two catchers from the D.R. [They had] really good abilities, but they never learned the language. They spent nine years in the minor leagues, and we can't put them in the majors because they can't speak English. Nothing! How is a catcher in charge of everything going to handle a pitcher? How's he going to answer the manager when he's asked 'How's his stuff?' Or, how is he going to give orders?"[41]

Race

It is difficult to get across to the rookies that what they call racial heterogeneity would in the United States be called racial homogeneity. Dominicans are given to racial hair splitting: in their social scheme a person can disdain those who are darker and be disdained in turn by those who are lighter. Dominicans are incredulous that in the United States one is either black or white (lighter-skinned Dominicans are afraid to believe this—it means they would lose their advantage in the United States—and darker-skinned Dominicans can barely conceal their glee). Racial intolerance is also more pronounced in the United States than in the Dominican Republic. While some lighter-skinned Hispanics played professional baseball in the United States before the game was integrated in 1947,[42] the mulattos who make up the overwhelming majority of the Dominican Republic could not.

Dominican players of the late 1950s and early 1960s faced the same racism as their black American counterparts did: "We were not used to [racism]. We didn't know about it here. Sometimes [in the United States] you go into a restaurant and they just didn't serve you. They didn't say nothing, and they didn't serve you. That's why a lotta guys came back here."[43] According to another player, who left baseball because of his experiences in the American minor leagues in the 1950s: "I had a hard time because I was the only black there. Then, they looked for another one. And only so many blacks could play on a team. In spring training we had a bunch of good ballplayers, good black players . . . We had fifteen minor league teams in the franchise, but only two blacks could go on each team. As soon as you see three blacks, you know one of them is gonna go." Still another player recalled:

> In Florida, I played in the Northern League. I played and when
> I went the manager said, "They gonna yell a lot of things at you.

Put cotton in your ears." They took me to the black section [to
live]. I introduced myself as a ballplayer, and the people said,
"Where you gonna play?" When I told them where they said,
"No no, you made a mistake. No black ballplayers ever played
here." I told them, "You go tonight, and you gonna see." So
then, all of these blacks packed into the stands to see this Black
ballplayer play . . . Yes, the racism was a problem. I couldn't eat
with white players. When I went home [to the Dominican Re-
public] they couldn't believe what I told them. I had to take over
[news]papers to show them.[44]

Overt segregation is unconstitutional, but contemporary Dominicans
still encounter racism. One of the rookies in a group at the camp remarked openly that a much darker friend had been ill treated during his
baseball foray in the United States. The other members of the group
then discoursed on their own experiences, some also negative while
others were more positive:

I could feel it, but I can't say I had much difficulty from it.
Blacks like us much more than white ballplayers, and we never
room with whites on my team.[45]

In the USA there is big racism. In the places I played I felt it, but I
didn't pay attention to it. I ignored the players that didn't like me,
and they didn't speak to me. Sometimes they called us with deni-
grating words. They thought we couldn't understand, but I did.
In the first year I used to fight a lot, but now I've changed.[46]

People are nice to Dominican players. They really like
Dominicans.[47]

After fifteen days people were very fond of Negrín and me. All
the Americans were really nice to us. We lived in a house with
Americans.[48]

While there was no consensus on racism, there were enough comments about it to warrant my making it a topic of discussion in class at
the academy. Somehow it was sobering to the lighter-skinned players for
them to realize that they might be the targets of racial slurs as easily as
they could inflict them on others.

The Dominican Drug Line

Hard numbers are elusive, but impressionistic data from reliable sources
suggest that the threat of losing Dominican ballplayers to drugs is real
and growing. Drug abuse among ballplayers was mentioned to me in

interviews both by Dominicans who played in the United States in the late 1960s and by current players: "The players drop [amphetamines] in their coffee, sometimes in their beer, and that makes them fly. I know this because I see these pills all over the clubhouse." [49]

In early 1989 the Dominican pitcher Pascual Pérez was temporarily suspended for substance abuse, but players who use drugs are only a small part of the problem: that on occasion drug traffickers recruit players for dealing in drugs is far more threatening. One evening when I was going through photographs with a scout in his living room, we came across a picture taken in 1982 of four young men, all smiling and holding their bats. The men belonged to a championship Dominican team that had gone to Canada. When I asked the scout what the men were doing now he told me that one played professionally in the United States in class AA of the minor leagues, two continued to play amateur ball, and one, a brilliant player, had given up baseball to sell drugs in New York. The scout even said that drug peddlers have been known occasionally to go after Dominican ballplayers at the baseball camps in Florida. For players faced with a hard life, drug money can be a seductive alternative to peddling fruit in Santo Domingo or working the cane fields.

Many players who make it to the United States decide to lose themselves there. Those in the camps who have played there and returned to the Dominican Republic freely suggest to others that they remain in the United States, even if they must do so illegally: "Guys who get released don't come back [to Santo Domingo]. They can't do much here. They usually go to New York City. They ask me, 'What should I do?' I say, 'How much can you earn if you go back, three hundred pesos a month? 350 maybe?' Then they usually say, 'I'm going to New York.'" [50]

The Language Lesson

I monitored the English classes offered by the Dodgers in Campo Las Palmas at various times during 1988–89. There were two instructors during that time. The Dodgers had been using instructors from Guerra, which is nearby. Santo Domingo has established schools and instructors, but it is very difficult for a remote academy like Campo Las Palmas to use them: the time and money that an instructor has to spend to get from Santo Domingo to the academy outweighs his salary.

The problem with using an established English program at a baseball academy is that instructors from outside the academy will make assumptions about teaching the language that will not be tenable. First, the educational level of the baseball prospect is much lower than that of

the student to whom the conventional teacher is accustomed. Second, the motivation to learn English is generally lower at the baseball academy: the student works a full day and is tired by the time classes begin; the instructor may not be able to teach at any other time. Finally, the duration of a prospect's stay at the camp may not correspond to the duration of an established course of study.

When I observed one conventional attempt at language instruction, I found the curriculum and teaching strategy completely irrelevant to the boys' needs and the execution counterproductive. The incongruity of having to sit in a classroom for an hour at the end of a long, hard day of physical exercise is not lost on the players. They saunter in, notebooks in hand, their entrance always accompanied by a verbal or physical signature. One particularly large and imposing-looking student makes a point of walking too close to the teacher when he arrives, in an apparent attempt to intimidate. Another grabs his crotch and makes a comment about a girl in Guerra. This behavior reflects the lack of control that the teacher has of his class, and the feeling of the students that the class is not at all important. Although on the verge of a high-paying career, most have long since given up on education.

Nevertheless the class begins, and after ten or fifteen minutes everyone is present. The teacher has been going through a list of vocabulary. Sometimes the vocabulary is pertinent, at other times it is not. At one class meeting the teacher jotted down the following words on the board: real estate agency (written "real state agency"), barber shop, university, laundry, bridge. These words are certainly not relevant to the players' immediate needs. The teacher then had the students construct sentences about asking directions. This is a good idea, but the questions were phrased inappropriately ("Excuse me, which bus do I take to the university?" and "Is there a library near here?"), as were the answers (the reply to the question about the library, "Yes, there is one around the corner," implied that libraries are as common as newsstands in Manhattan). The boys were just mouthing the questions and answers with no real comprehension. By this time I had seen the boys for a year and knew how much English they had mastered, and I could tell that this approach to teaching them English was a waste of time. What would have been appropriate for a regular student body or for people who were embarking on a long-term plan to master the language was not working with these boys. They simply did not care that the "eraser is under the table." They had to learn how to function in a strange and somewhat frightening environment, and they had to learn soon.

What is needed is a curriculum especially designed for the baseball prospect. Many organizations realize this and try to design their own, but unfortunately this is often nothing more than a photocopied list of baseball terms. One such list that I looked at included the baseball phrases "cut it off," "I got it," and "get back," the names for parts of the baseball uniform, various greetings ("How are you?"), and words found on street signs. The intention was to link the learning of English to the occupation of the students, but the execution was pitifully inadequate and far too limiting.

I put together a curriculum that tried to fill the gap between conventional language instruction and the needs of ballplayers. My hope was to teach the players a few useful verbs in the present tense, by means of simple sentences that the players might use in everyday social situations. I would do this not through constant repetition, which the boys obviously loathed, but through role playing. Since the length of time that a player spends in Campo Las Palmas is fairly unpredictable, I decided to design the course with the assumption that the student's stay would be short.

I constructed four social situations in which the boys would be likely to find themselves in the minor leagues. In each situation there were at least two roles, one of which was played by the ballplayer, and the dialogue was not only realistic but included much cultural information.[51] My assistant and I would go through each dialogue acting out the parts, and then have the players do this. Since the players knew these were situations they might encounter, they paid close attention. When the players had practiced a dialogue a few times and felt comfortable with it, they would exchange roles: the customer in a restaurant would become the waiter, the waiter would become the customer. By this time my assistant and I noticed that some of the brighter players were trying to deviate from the dialogue, which provided welcome relief and was encouraged by us. This allowed the slower students to stick to the dialogue as written, while the faster ones could try new combinations of responses. The results were very gratifying. The boys who had been clownish and had not taken the program seriously improved, and those who were motivated became that much more conversant with English. One problem I noted was that for the most part the ones who were doing best in class were, alas, not doing the best on the field; and the best players were the furthest behind linguistically. Future generations of the program would have to take this into account. Unfortunately the program fell apart after I left. A new instructor was hired, one who used the traditional methods, and when I returned in early 1989 I saw that the boys had reverted to their clownish, unresponsive, and irreverent behavior. I am now formulating a proposal to the Dodgers based on my experiment.

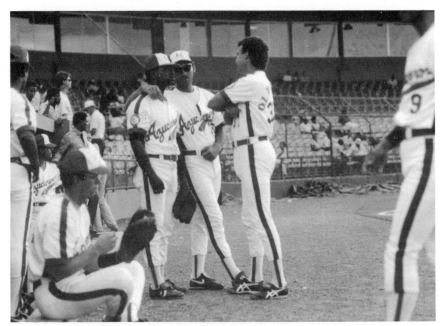

1. La Romana players chatting before a game. The casual style of social interaction so much a part of Latino culture is in evidence in baseball as well.

2. A professional game at Quisqueya Stadium in Santo Domingo. The oldest and most prestigious baseball stadium in the country, Quisqueya is the home to both professional teams in the capital, the Licey Tigers and the Escogido Lions.

3. Many North American baseball terms are used in the Dominican Republic. Changes in pronunciation sometimes result in humorous variations, as at this takeout store near Quisqueya Stadium.

4. Houston Astro rookies.

5. One of the infamous vendors at Quisqueya Stadium, where one can run up a tab or see a vendor perform a merengue or an instant replay.

6. A young boy from San Pedro de Macorís holds a baseball mitt fashioned from a paper milk carton. This makeshift mitt symbolizes better than anything the Dominican determination to succeed against all odds.

7. A young Escogido fan seems unmoved by the excitement of a championship game.

8. Dominican baseball is a study in the contrast between old and new. Here bright young stars of the future play near a refinery while cattle graze just outside the foul lines.

9. In the summer of 1989 the Toronto Blue Jays had five Dominican players on their major league club. From left: Manny Lee, Nelson Liriano, coach Winston Llenas, Silvestre Campusano, Tony Fernández, George Bell.

10. The Dominicans call it "sucking cane," and many, like this young boy outside San Pedro de Macorís, are forced to do it because they lack other affordable sources of nutrition.

11. In a remote ballpark near a sugar refinery, Tom Lasorda, manager of the Los Angeles Dodgers, talks with the former major league pitcher Joaquín Andujar.

12. At the stadium one is likely to encounter such great players of the past as Juan Marichal, who pitched brilliantly for the San Francisco Giants and is now in the baseball Hall of Fame.

13. The entrance to the Dodger academy, Campo Las Palmas, the most extravagantly built and complete facility of its kind in the Dominican republic.

14. Ralph Avila, head of Campo Las Palmas.

The Head Case

It is not clear how many Latin American players are lost to major league teams—the teams are loath to disclose figures that might reflect poorly on their program—but the directors I have spoken to say it is a serious concern. One major league director of scouting said the attrition rate for two teams he knew about was 30 percent. Players fail for a variety of reasons, some of which have nothing to do with poor playing skills. One often hears the term "head case" applied to Latino players who fail or who do not reach their potential.

The term describes a player whose behavior is excessive, unpredictable, unconventional, and difficult for the organization to control. It covers a wide range of personality types. Among those who could be considered head cases are George Bell, outfielder for the Toronto Blue Jays, because of his ill temper; Pascual Pérez, pitcher for the New York Yankees, who is widely regarded as a "goofball"; and Joaquín Andujar, former pitcher for the St. Louis Cardinals, because of his prodigious outbursts of temper. But people in baseball use the term "head case" too inclusively, and some are too willing to call a Latino player a head case simply because he is a product of a culture that is foreign to them.

When does the label cease to be applicable? Can it be lost or altered over time? And how does one differentiate cultural differences from personality problems? In my view the important distinction is between players whose unconventional behavior affects their performance on the field and those who are able to keep them separate.

Perhaps the most difficult loss for a major league team is that of a prospect with all the skills who becomes a "head case": after being painstakingly brought up the organizational ladder he falters for reasons having nothing to do with playing but rather because of social dislocation or real psychological problems. The problem is manifested in a variety of ways. A troubled young man may undergo a mood shift and become sullen and uncommunicative, or highly agitated, or perhaps swing between excitability and moodiness. The player resists coaching and managerial decisions, at times becomes ungovernable, and soon begins to play erratically on the field. He is forever grumbling and expressing dissatisfaction, and team morale suffers. The organization is frustrated because of the hopes it has pinned on the player and the money it has invested in his future. It is important, however, to distinguish the point at which the term "head case" ceases to apply to this sort of behavior.

The most extreme head case I encountered during my stay in the Dominican Republic was a young Dominican who had experienced a rise that was all too rapid. The swiftness of his success coupled with his immaturity led to an emotional breakdown. The player had been taken under the wing of several countrymen who had already made it in the United States. Early one season he was suddenly and dramatically called up to the parent club because of injuries to a regular player. An impressive rookie season followed, and it looked to all concerned as if a major baseball talent was emerging. The following winter he played in the Dominican league, but he was uncoachable. The fans booed him, which so rattled the young player that he committed an egregious error that led to a scuffle with some fans. He was arrested and jailed, and the parent club had to come to his aid. When he walked out of his cell resplendent in gold chains and rings, one police officer wanted to jail him again just to get at his jewelry; he was stopped by a substantial bribe.

The young man went through cycles of self-blame and arrogance. The team spent money on a psychiatrist, but to no avail. The skills that got him to the majors deteriorated as he independently decided to pursue hitting strategies totally different from those that had brought him success. The decline in his batting average did nothing to deter him. In an attempt to build his confidence one coach told him he could be the next Ozzie Smith (the all-star shortstop for the St. Louis Cardinals); this plan backfired when the player began fielding one-handed and made dozens of errors. When the team's Latin American coaches were asked to straighten him out they did not put up with his arrogance; the young man promptly began crying that no one loved him. He has since been traded.

The troubles of the Toronto Blue Jays made public in spring 1989 are also illustrative of the use of the term "head case." Epy Guerrero, scout for the Toronto Blue Jays, became disgusted with the problems that the players he signed had with the parent club: "They say he [the Dominican infielder Jimy Kelly] has a bad attitude and can't get along with managers. And he thinks everybody is against him . . . But he's not the only Latin kid who wants out. All the Dominican kids have jumped all over me. They all have a complaint of some kind."[52] The Blue Jays were accusing Kelly of being a head case, but he countered with numerous charges that it was in fact the team that was at fault. This was a rare instance of a team being accused of using a label to control a player (see chapter 5).

Guerrero created a stir in spring training with his contention that Toronto did not treat Latin American players as well as North American players (see chapter 5). He had been receiving a considerable amount of press, having appeared on the television show "West 57th Street" and in *People*. This gave him a high degree of visibility, and the Blue Jays had

to take him seriously; their reputation would be severely damaged if
Guerrero's charges were borne out. Some baseball people in the Dominican Republic feel that Guerrero simply shot from the lip, as he is
known periodically to do; I know of at least one other time when he had
created a controversy by exaggerating a claim. Perhaps Guerrero was
calling attention to real organizational shortcomings on the part of the
Blue Jays—or perhaps he was himself acting the part of a head case.
Guerrero had placed himself at risk to call attention to a situation that
he and others felt was abusive. The Blue Jays denied the charge and
quietly went about trying to bury the incident; to my knowledge little of
substance has been done to clear up the matter.

Other young men are womanizers who carry on to the point of legal
and psychological distraction, or brilliant prospects who simply think
they know best what they need to do. I was told of some players who
began humbly enough in the Florida Rookie Leagues, where they impressed their coaches with offensive displays. Each year they moved up
a notch as they continued to improve; then, suddenly and almost without warning, they seemed to become full of themselves and stopped
taking managerial advice. Attorneys for major league clubs and other
organizational officials know only too well how much energy they must
expend to extricate players from embarrassing situations that they have
themselves created. The Dominican outfielder Luis Polonia, the unfortunate target of a morals charge when he was a member of the New York
Yankees, was eventually traded to the California Angels; another Dominican player, a rookie who was confronted by a woman with whom
he had had a casual liaison, was intimidated into marrying her in front
of his teammates.

Perhaps no one better typifies the head case than Pérez. Like many
head cases, he has had an extremely uneven career. In late 1982 and
1983 he pitched effectively for the Atlanta Braves, winning nineteen
games and losing only twelve. After spending three months in prison in
the Dominican Republic in 1984 he rejoined the team and picked up
where he had left off. But he became involved soon after in an irrational
"bean ball" war with the pitching staff of the San Diego Padres. From
that time his career quickly declined, and in 1985 he won one game
and lost thirteen. Two years later he was signed by the Montreal Expos,
and although he returned to form by winning seven games and losing
none in 1987 and winning twelve while losing only eight in the following year, he again declined in 1989.

Pérez has no shortage of detractors. Opposing players have commented on how his "hot dogging" has prompted them to think violent
thoughts. Dave LaPoint, pitcher for the Yankees, recalled: "Guys wanted

to bounce balls off Pascual's knees, if not his skull." Teammates joked about him derisively, and once weighed his gold jewelry when he was otherwise disposed. Managers upbraided him for ignoring signs, showing up late for games, and on one infamous occasion not showing up at all. Pérez's behavior was intended to create distance between himself and those around him; the effect was to increase his cultural isolation, distract him from his job, and eventually lead to ineptitude.

Head Cases and Cultural Stereotypes

Not all head cases are Latino. Dennis "Oil Can" Boyd, now pitching for Montreal, bobs about the pitcher's mound and holds animated conversations with himself. Jimmy Piersall, who played outfield for the Boston Red Sox and was the most celebrated head case of his time, suffered a nervous breakdown and eventually wrote a book about it. But Latino players are labeled head cases to a disproportionate degree.

Both player and organization need to examine their goals and the means they use to achieve them—separately and jointly. Player and organization are by no means equal: the player is much more dependent on the team than the team is on him, and he has much more to lose should he fail. But there are some things the player can do to redress the balance in his favor.

A ballplayer is three things: an individual, a member of a socioeconomic group, and a member of a cultural group. Most baseball clubs see the ballplayer only as the first of these and reward and punish him accordingly. They tend to divide the Latino players into two categories: the head cases and what I call the heads of the class. The heads of the class are players whose behavior is exemplary, who respond with the same equanimity to adulation and insult, success and hardship. Some of these players are exuberant in their love for the game and minimize its difficulties; among them are Minnie Minoso, an outstanding player for the Chicago White Sox in the 1960s, and Tony Peña of the Boston Red Sox. Other heads of the class are more serious, like the shortstops Tony Fernández of the Blue Jays and Alfredo Griffin of the Dodgers.

While most of the teams know that the greater number of their Latino rookies come from poor backgrounds, they often assume that this will become insignificant when the player reaches North America, or even dismiss it as insignificant in the first place. Unfortunately this is not often the case: even if a rookie's family background is sufficiently normal for his ego to have undergone healthy development, extreme poverty is likely to have damaged it.

One young rookie who had all the tools for success provides an example. Thrown out of his parents' shanty at the age of eight, he took to living where he could (like many *tigeritos*, or street urchins), in this instance under the grandstand at the stadium in his town. There he lived hand to mouth, at night collecting plastic soda and beer cups that he would wash and resell the next day. He lived this way for nine years, among thieves and rats, at the same time honing his baseball talents. The scouts spotted his abilities by the time he was seventeen. When word of their interest got back to the boy's parents, they insisted on rebuilding their familial tie and asked their son to move into the chicken shed behind their home. So starved was the boy for affection that he was willing to take even this rather than real love. When the boy signed, his father took his signing bonus, and when he was given a sports jacket to wear in the United States even this was taken away, but the son was gratified because now he was worth stealing from. Insecurities such as his make for an uncertain present and future. There can be little doubt that social and economic pressures can derail even the most talented rookies.

Poverty increases the pressure to succeed in the major leagues. Not only does a player's family depend on his success but often his entire community does as well, and since Dominican ballplayers have been so talented the expectations are high. Jaime Torres, an agent for Latino players in the United States, says that for most of his clients high status is intoxicating and fear of failure a nightmare: "There's always that status . . . it's very prestigious [playing in the United States]. But unfortunately, in the Dominican Republic when a player gets released, you wouldn't believe the shame. You're worthless. This is a failure. He was given the opportunity and he failed." [53]

To have come from a poor background, possibly rural, and to be uneducated makes the transition to the United States difficult. The anxiety not only affects the caliber of a rookie's playing but may even prevent him from playing. For a Dominican eighteen-year-old, homesickness is much graver than for his North American counterpart heading off to college. It is compounded by serious doubts and often a faltering sense of self-esteem. The player may simply leave the game if his team does not offer him the support he needs.

Among the cultural factors that come into play are two Latino male character traits, *machismo* and *personalismo*, which contribute to an inflated sense of self-worth, self-centeredness, and often a sense of entitlement. One sees these traits manifested in an excessive swaggering and cockiness, and an exaggerated.male pride that is easily slighted. In Dominican baseball the psychological bubble may be inflated by initial success, then burst when the parent club demands more than the player is prepared to give, or when the fans and the press at home call the player to task. Humble origins can either exacerbate personalismo or temper it (as they did with Roberto Clemente, the great Puerto Rican outfielder now in the baseball Hall of Fame). For the insecure, setbacks are not taken lightly, and they result in feelings of persecution and hypersensitivity.

North American athletes are certainly just as likely as Latin Americans to exhibit hypermasculine behavior, but in Latin America machismo linked with personalismo is a deeply embedded cultural form. Historically it is manifest in the Latin American *caudillo*, the institutionalized archetypes of Don Juan and the overindulged son, and the rock-hard sexism of Latino society. The poor seek to follow the code every bit as much as members of the landed aristocracy do, but with less success; their posturing is more hollow. The player of humble roots is more sensitive to criticism from the press, management, and fans, and more likely to act up should he be threatened. For the Dominican player, or indeed for any Latin American player, the combination of rapid career advancement, possibly weak ego development, machismo, and cultural dislocation can precipitate a fall. One player who succumbed to one revealed some of his empty boastfulness when he declared: "Before, nobody back home knew who I was; they didn't talk to me. Now the big people, the guys with a lot of money, always say hi. They seen me in the playoffs. They know me." [54]

All this makes for a young player barely able to cope with success on the field, and virtually doomed when faced with setbacks off the field. A slump in performance can bring about a cycle of self-blame and erratic, moody, sullen behavior that reinforces the poor performance. Matters are often made even worse when a player has not been brought up through the minor leagues (Jimy Kelly of the Blue Jays is an example).

How Organizations Handle Latino Rookies

The conclusion reached by many Dodger administrators like Campanis and Avila—that Latino players are a bit emotionally immature—offers an insight into the behavioral problems faced by organizations as well as by players. The age at which many Dominican rookies are signed, seventeen or even younger, may be at the root of this. Many who have played in North America complain about having gone there too young. One who went to Montana at the age of sixteen said: "I was young. I could have used more education to be better prepared to live in the

United States." And Juan Samuel of the Dodgers once told a reporter:
"Kids are signing too young because clubs feel if they don't sign them
now, somebody else will come in tomorrow and sign them. When I was
coming [to the majors], I don't think there were five scouts in the Dominican. It's going to reach a point where they're going to have to put
some restrictions on signing them. I'd like to see them have to finish
high school or a commitment to finish in this country . . . They can
sign at any age. And even if he finished school there, there are few jobs
for him when he finishes. Everyone is trying to get out of the country,
and that's what forces kids to sign too young." [55]

Organizations see things differently. They find signing players at so
early an age cost-effective, since players are more expensive when they
are more seasoned. Minor league directors sometimes attempt to justify
the practice by saying that younger players adjust more easily to life and
the style of play in North America.

The academies can alleviate these problems if they offer sufficient
preparation to their students. The Dodgers, the Blue Jays, and the
White Sox are among those that do. But most major league teams see
their academies as little more than baseball hothouses in which athletic
skills are taught and other areas ignored.

A weak support system in North America compounds the problems of
adjusting to a different culture. Matters would be much improved if a
Latino or Spanish-speaking counselor were available to help the rookies, or if the English-speaking staff were more knowledgeable about Latino culture and society: "In the minors they give you leaflets with words
such as how to call the ball, how to say 'cutoff,' 'strike,' and outside stuff
such as how to order in restaurants . . . but us Latinos always have a
fear that we will put our foot in our mouth and everyone will laugh." [56]

Another way organizations can hinder their players' development is
by labeling them. A player who carries the stigma of the head case does
not easily lose it. His opposite, the player at the head of the class, is
more common and very quickly categorized. One such player, who has
since gone on to the major leagues, while in the Dominican Republic
set the standard for behavior on and off the field. He possessed the most
sought-after qualities—talent, intelligence, and temperament: "He's
smart, but he's smart in baseball. He got a normal education, maybe
sixth or seventh grade. He comes from a good family. He's got common
sense. He can analyze the game. He's nineteen, but he knows what he's
doing wrong. If you have a good coach, you can advance quickly . . .
You gotta convince the player he's doing something wrong before you
can teach him. R—— is the type of person you can coach." [57]

The bipolar view of players held by most baseball organizations is not especially valid or useful. Some players who are perhaps too aggressive or belligerent are labeled head cases even though their unconventional behavior does not affect their play on the field. One player of this type is George Bell of the Blue Jays. Bell is a very difficult man to deal with: he bullies players, the press, and outsiders alike, and his behavior at times verges on the sociopathic. But Bell nevertheless plays to the fullest of his abilities. He compartmentalizes his problems as much as any player can be expected to do.

The headstrong Latino player has always been seen as a cultural type. Rubén Gómez, the Puerto Rican major league pitcher of the 1950s and 1960s, was known by the nickname "Divine crazy." He once attacked a manager for wrongfully fining him. Those who condemned him never took into account that he came from an impoverished family where people stood up for their rights, especially if they felt they were unjustifiably deprived of their money. But the incident plagued Gómez throughout his career, and he was repeatedly traded and hounded. His behavior never affected his play, however, and he had a successful career as a journeyman.

The great outfielder Roberto Clemente was perhaps the epitome of the headstrong player. Had he been any less talented his volatile personality would have been less tolerated, and he would no doubt have been stigmatized as many other outspoken Latino and African-American players have been.

An organization often sees less compliant behavior as sufficient grounds for being traded or for having one's movement through the organization held up. At best this is cultural insensitivity and intolerance, at worst systematic persecution.

Manipulating the Labels

Latino players are often painfully aware of the labeling system and will go to extremes to avoid it. Sometimes the fear of being labeled prompts a player to play in pain, even to the point of risking an injury that will threaten his career. One rookie at Campo Las Palmas played for more than two weeks with a broken wrist before being put on the disabled list. Perhaps he could not distinguish a slight injury from a serious one, but it is also possible that he did not want to be seen as a complainer.

Alfredo Griffin of the Dodgers recalled the advice he had been given early in his career by Rod Carew, a fellow Latino: "He tells us, you got to show that you can play every day. He said if we wanted to make it, we could give them no excuse to get rid of us. That is what I live by." [58]

Playing in pain also dovetails nicely with Latino notions of machismo. One Latino player said of an injured teammate: "He's a Dominican. He grew up on the streets, he has taken a lot more pain than
people can imagine. But he will keep everything to himself. He tells
nobody nothing. He plays hard, and you have to force him to stop." [59]

Back in the minor leagues the rookies quickly conform to this way of
thinking. At times some will not even make their legitimate needs
known for fear of being labeled. Some rookies badly in need of shoes,
for example, will play in pain rather than ask for new ones. [60]

The trade or demotion so widely feared by players can on occasion
work to their advantage. Sometimes a change of scenery can mature a
player as much as the passage of time can. Julio Franco offers a good
example of this. In his years with the Cleveland Indians he was widely
seen as difficult, brash, uncooperative—the classic Latino head case—
although his performance on the field was always impressive. He had a
bad reputation in the press, which bred in him a hostility toward journalists that he retained for some time: "Don't read newspapers. You
make a mistake and it will always haunt you. They're always waiting for
you to make another mistake . . . If you're a Latin ballplayer in the
U.S.A. learn to ignore things." [61]

Franco's behavior, and the label he was given, no doubt led to his
being traded to the Texas Rangers. But once there he changed from
being a head case to being at the head of the class. He now counsels
other young Latinos to get their temper under control. Clearly several
things played a role in Franco's behavior: culture (personalismo and
machismo), socioeconomic factors, a later maturation, premature entry
into the United States, and personality. And just as clearly the organization that brought him to the United States had little understanding of
cultural and social issues, prepared him poorly, promoted him too
quickly, and gave him insufficient help once he was in the United
States. A patient team, one that is not given to rushing talent through
the system, will have a better player, a better reputation in the player's
homeland, and a better chance of succeeding as a franchise.

The Avila Story: An Outsider on the Inside Track

Both early in my field work and at the end of it I was told by various
people that if I wanted to know about baseball in the Dominican Republic I would have to talk to Ralph Avila. At first I laughed this off,
thinking that I was being passed along from one respondent to another,
as one often is in field work. But by the time I finished my study I had

come to realize that Avila probably was the best baseball mind in the country, and also the most problematic.

Avila is a Cuban, a naturalized American citizen, working for an American company while living in the Dominican Republic. He is the outsider, sent by the Americans: part welcomed, part feared, and part trusted. Such a fragmented national identity might cause problems for others, but Avila has skillfully used his diverse background to fashion a life for himself that is at once baseball and personal. Avila, fifty-nine years old, is a roly-poly, bespectacled man who looks like a beardless Santa Claus. He is a practical joker. He curses when he has to drink horse-tail tea each day,[62] and lights up when the conversation turns to Afro-Cuban music. He struts around his academy like a feudal lord. He is feared by baseball people in the Dominican Republic, held in patriarchal awe by the rookies in Campo Las Palmas, depended on by the Los Angeles Dodgers, and respected by everyone connected with the game. His wife calls him "Avila."

His mildness, his even temper, last only as long as the game is not on the line, or as long as someone does not betray him. Otherwise Avila becomes Attila, and the gentle-looking grandfather becomes a pit bull. It does not take much for Avila to feel betrayed: someone trying to shirk responsibility or work, slander, hypocrisy—all are things that Avila cannot tolerate.

The success of Avila validates a notion of mine: that while baseball and politics may mix in the United States, in Latin America baseball and radical politics mix even more readily. Not only is Fidel Castro a baseball fan of the first order, but his long-time relationship with Ted Turner, the very embodiment of capitalism, is rooted in his love for the game. Gil Joseph has pointed out the radical political role that baseball came to play in the early twentieth century in the Yucatán Peninsula.[63] Nicaragua provides further examples. Daniel Ortega, the former Sandinista president of Nicaragua, is an avid follower of the Baltimore Orioles, and he is often photographed wearing a Mets cap. That contras and Sandinistas should be able to agree on anything is newsworthy, but baseball has always proven to be the cultural form that crosses political lines. When Nicaragua lost in a recent international baseball competition, one Sandinista felt the loss so deeply that he remarked, "It was so sad, even the contras cried." As beleaguered as Nicaragua may be, it still considers itself a land of baseball fanatics that will tolerate all sorts of shortages and government interference in the cause of revolution, but absolutely no interference in the broadcasting of major league games. Similarly Cubans living in the United States and their compatriots at home use baseball as a vehicle through which political tension is expressed and even mediated.

Ralph Avila embodies as well as anyone the mixture of radical politics and baseball. His life certainly attests to this, but I was nevertheless
jolted by his unhesitating response to my question about what he might
be doing if he were not in baseball: "I'd be somewhere in Nicaragua."
"Somewhere" told it all (he would be working for the contras).

In his life Avila has seemingly gone from one end of the Latin American political spectrum to the other, fighting first on the side of Castro
and then against him. One of the first things that I learned about him
was that he had taken part in the Bay of Pigs invasion. Most Americans
would assume that anyone involved in this debacle was to the right of
Genghis Khan. But Avila cannot be judged by American political standards; in Latin America people often carry a mixed bag of political principles. For in talking about his anti-Castroism Avila told me that he had
also driven the lead jeep in Che Guevara's triumphant march to Havana
in 1959. I wondered how anyone could move so quickly from left to
right. Was Avila as complete a counter-revolutionary as he had once
been a revolutionary?

The answer lies in not thinking of left and right as fixed and mutually
exclusive categories. For the Latin American perhaps more than for the
North American, political affinity is often closely bound up with personality; and since politics tends to be the province of men, in Latin
America it becomes associated with machismo. Avila's account of his
role in the ouster of Fulgencio Batista displayed a blend of political
shrewdness and machismo (indeed Avila's nickname in Cuba was "Ma-
cho"). He respected Guevara for having been in combat and disdained
Castro for not having been: "He was a legend. He was not like Castro.
Che fought on the front. He was first to fire. Even in going into Havana,
when Che was in the tank he didn't wanna be there. We made him sit in
the tank. Castro, he was always in back."[64]

Avila said on more than one occasion that what validated Guevara
was his bravery, not his politics: "People knew he was a communist. We
knew he was a lefty kinda guy, but he had courage, and he took care of
people." Avila was a member of an anti-Batista group (Juventud Obrera
Católica—Young Catholic Workers) that formed part of a united front.
The group was particularly militant and at one time sought to assassi-
nate Batista. In Avila's rendering of the events, Castro wanted to join in
the action against Batista but the group was cool toward him. Castro
then launched his own attack on the Moncado barracks a full two weeks
earlier than originally planned, foiling the assassination plans. From
this point on Avila opposed Castro. But Avila based his politics on an
odd combination of idealism, pragmatism, and personality. He ended
up joining the united front that formed under the leadership of Castro
because "there was nothing else you could do. He was the only one

around." Eliminating Batista was more pressing to all than communism or capitalism.

The struggle against Batista was waged by small bands of guerrillas in the mountains, in the countryside, and in the cities. While life was getting more oppressive and dangerous for the radicals, the national game—baseball—continued to flourish. Professional baseball was still being played throughout the revolution, and Avila had found another reason to keep playing semiprofessionally: "Because you could travel around more freely in buses and trucks, we would dress in our baseball uniforms from our semipro teams. And if Batista's soldiers stopped you on your way to making a [political] action we could declare ourselves a team traveling on business, to a game. They didn't stop baseball buses."[65]

Eugenics and Egalitarianism

The coexistence of opposing traits in Avila's personality is perhaps most clearly expressed in his views on eugenics and egalitarianism. There is an elitism inherent in viewing things eugenically: racial characteristics are assigned cultural values and then placed in a social hierarchy. Such schemes often lead to the elevation of one group over another on the basis of racial characteristics. In baseball some criteria used to assess a prospect's potential are based on eugenic notions. Baseball people see certain body types as prerequisites of success in the game (for example, pitchers should be tall, lean, and long-limbed), and it is a small step from these generalizations to eugenics and race psychology. Often I have heard highly respected baseball men insist that Mexico produces better pitchers than other countries because of the number of Indians in the Mexican population: "Who better than an Indian on the mound? They can concentrate better than other people."

In the Dominican Republic many of these baseball men view the best talent coming out of the refineries as the product of black genes. They seem to be subscribing to the biological principle of heterosis, or hybrid vigor, according to which the offspring of hybrid parents will be stronger than the parents. Avila shares some of these views: "It's always that way when you first mix black and Spanish; but after the first generation there is no kick left." But although these views often lead to racism, Avila is as far from being a racist as one can be. He is in fact staunchly egalitarian, a result of his father's influence: "In my father's house, our helpers ate with us, right at the table, same food as us. In my house now, Lina [a cook employed by Avila's wife, Gloria] is in our family. We go to movies, everything together."[66]

Ralph's father married up. His wife had inherited a small sugar cane plantation, which he took over after they were married; he worked it hard, personally and not like a patron. And when he hired black work-ers they were treated with dignity. He and his family appreciated their material good fortune, but unlike the landed gentry they did not see themselves as socially superior: "We were less poor than the others." From an early age Avila had learned from his father the value of hard work and the essence of sharing : "Mine was the first bicycle in town. I remember I didn't want anyone to ride it, but I was made to share it with the other [black] kids. My father said, 'You were playing with them before, you share with them now.' That was the way he taught us, to always share." [67]

Once yellow fever struck his town, killing forty-one children. Ralph's grandmother told both her son and her grandson to avoid traveling through the shantytown when they went to the ballpark. Both loved to take this route, since the old women would give them coffee and cookies as they passed. Ralph's father said that under no conditions would they stop. "If God wants [someone] then he'll take him no matter what you do." Worried about what message avoiding the poor in a time of peril would send to those less fortunate, Ralph's father continued to take their favorite route to the ballfield.

Ralph's father successfully communicated to his son the maxim "There but for the grace of God go I." Years later, when Ralph moved his own family from Miami to Santo Domingo and one of his sons had a difficult time adjusting to life there, Ralph asked his son whether he thought himself superior to the people among whom he now lived. His son replied that things were quite the contrary: he was so appalled at the poverty he saw that he was compelled to deny it, to block it from his consciousness. Avila was reassured that what he had feared might be racism on the part of his son was in fact a discomfort with suffering, much like his own.

Dodger Blue and Through

It remains difficult to reconcile the disparate sides of Ralph Avila, but his career in baseball provides a clue. Ralph's father managed a semi-professional team in their home town of Santa Maria in Cuba until he became ill, at which point leadership passed to Ralph (then twenty), who was still playing. At an age when most young men still harbor dreams of making it to the majors, Ralph embarked on a career in man-aging. After moving to Miami in 1959 he formed a baseball academy for young Cubans along with other Cuban-American ballplayers. He was now in a position to evaluate prospective ballplayers, and there was some interest in the baseball commissioner's office in hiring him as a scout. But in those days the scouting was an undervalued job (especially scouting in Latin America), and Avila could not afford to leave his job as a foreman in a sheet metal shop for a part-time job paying $1,000 a month.

Because it was so much a part of him it was a foregone conclusion that Avila would continue with baseball. The serendipitous possibility of working as a scout whetted his appetite, even though there was not yet a job he could afford to take. At the suggestion of his cousin, who knew Campanis, Avila asked the Dodgers whether there were opportunities for him to work as a scout and was encouraged to file reports on his own by Campanis, who probably did not expect him to follow through. But Avila was determined, and he began sending regular reports to the Dodgers: "One day [Campanis] called me and said 'I have to double-check some reports on some Cuban prospects.' When he told me the name of the ballplayers that he was coming to look at, and that everybody was so high on, I said 'I don't know why everybody is so high [on them] because I don't think they're that good . . . They're good college players, but not major league prospects.' We went to see the ballgame and he found out I was right . . . He called me more frequently. When the season was over he wrote me a really nice letter thanking me for everything I did for the Dodgers." [68]

Avila made the most of his opportunity. He impressed the Dodgers' management, first by shrugging off the polite rejection Campanis had given him, then by following up on the team's token offer that he send them reports, and finally by having the courage to disagree with powerful people in the organization. Campanis had found a person who would speak his mind and who was good at spotting talent. The die had been cast: Avila and the Los Angeles Dodgers would form a lifelong bond. Other, more rewarding contacts followed: "The next year Campanis sent Hugh Alexander from Oklahoma. We talked about the ballplayers, and I gave my opinion. I got more interested, but I wasn't making a penny. In fact, I was losing money 'cause I had to take off of work to go to the games . . . Hugh really liked me and taught me a lot. Finally Campanis decided to give me a part-time job." [69]

The relationship between Alexander and Avila was one of mutual respect. When Alexander later left to work with the Philadelphia Phillies, he tried to entice Avila to join him there. While others might have jumped at the opportunity to enhance their career, Avila's first impulse was one of loyalty to the people who had given him his first chance. He

would try to stay: "I said, 'Hugh, I really appreciate it. I'd love to work
for you. But I cannot do it. I got to tell Campanis. I cannot just quit the Dodgers; they gave me the break and I got to be honest. I got to call him and tell him that I got another offer. I got to get his permission.' I reported this to Campanis. He screamed and told me not to go."[70]

Apparently Avila's value and loyalty were recognized by Campanis, for in 1970 he was appointed a scout for Puerto Rico, Venezuela, the Dominican Republic, and all of southern Florida. Campanis "always liked Latin America," Avila recalls, and as his search for talent led him to focus more attention on the region (and especially on the Dominican Republic) he increased the influence and responsibilities of his new scout. Los Angeles had had a working agreement with Escogido for more than a dozen years when they decided to send Avila to Santo Domingo for the first time in 1971. Relations with Escogido had soured, and Avila's job was to establish ties with Licey. Thus began Avila's bond with the Dominican Republic: "At that time I liked what I saw. Great people. At that time they needed a lot of help in baseball, advice . . . In February Licey went to spring training and we signed a working agreement. I was coming here every month. Early in October I set up the training camp. And I stayed on to be Lasorda's coach and scout too."[71]

In 1974 Avila moved to Santo Domingo for what was intended to be a two-year assignment (one that continued into the 1990s). The duties he had as a scout and occasional coach for Licey expanded significantly when he started the baseball academy at Campo Las Palmas in 1981. He now has a staff that includes scouts and coaches, and he still makes periodic trips into the hinterlands to sign prospects.

Originally there was some reluctance to accept Avila. Apart from Monchín Pichardo, the head of Licey, Dominicans perceived Avila as an outsider. Suspicions were aroused by more than his foreignness: his outspokenness, which had always been an asset in his dealings with the Dodgers, was a drawback in the Dominican Republic, where the close-knit baseball people resented having an outsider call attention to their faults. They did value an American presence, however, and harbored a grudging respect for the baseball savvy of the Cubans: "The first four or five years here in the Dominican Republic, they didn't like me. I was Cuban, and I didn't agree with all the things that went on here. But now they see I'm doing a job; that I'm good with both black and white people, and they say, 'I was wrong with you. You looked so mean!'"[72]

Over the years Avila has taken on almost everybody in the Dominican baseball world: owners, managers, players, the press, and amateur baseball officials. What makes them even more furious than they would otherwise be is that Avila has usually been right. Avila has had periodic confrontations with journalists. He says sportswriters do not always spend the time they need to write meaningfully, and sometimes hurt players by dashing off carelessly thrown together stories without verifying their accuracy or considering their implications. Yet Avila is now on good terms with the press: he regularly exchanges the hat of an academy director for that of a television sportscaster in Santo Domingo, and members of the press respect his in-depth understanding of the game.

Avila knows that the press is not fully to blame for its own errors, since it has been reduced to its present state by a lack of support from the owners of professional clubs. As we sat in Quisqueya Stadium one day, I asked Avila why he thought attendance was down that year. He pointed around the stadium and told me that although it was "kids' day" children were nowhere to be seen. He said that given the lack of established stars who play winter baseball the press should be promoting events like kids' day more aggressively, but that because the press has been treated so shabbily by the owners it has little incentive to do so. Owners themselves have been lax about promoting events that draw fans to the park. When Avila managed Licey for a brief period he would hire buses to pick up children throughout the city. All they needed to get on board was a baseball uniform—any one would do. They would be given some treats, a tour, and a chance to watch their favorites from the bleachers; after the game they would be driven home. Avila says that most owners shy away from anything that cannot make money. This assessment is intended to rankle, and it is consistent with Avila's reputation as an outsider.

Amateur baseball is yet another area in which Avila has caused waves. When he turned his attention to amateur baseball in 1979, the Dominican Republic was the doormat of international amateur competition. Discipline is not valued particularly highly in Dominican baseball: each year the Dominican Republic enters a team in the Caribbean Series that is loaded with fine players and heavily favored, yet regularly loses because of the players' excesses off the diamond. Against the wishes of many people Avila was offered the chance to run the amateur program, which was preparing a team for the Pan American Games in Panama. There was a strong feeling among Dominican baseball people that the position should go to one of their own players. Avila was willing to take on the job only if it was agreed that everything would be done his way.

Avila ordered that each of the twenty-six provinces should select nine players and a coach, and all were invited to a tryout camp. The other amateur administrators and the press panicked, because what Avila was proposing meant cutting the amateur rosters drastically. Avila was

roundly insulted, and many Dominicans asked why a Cuban was in
charge of their team when there were so many qualified Dominicans. Avila ignored his critics and shocked everyone again by saying he would have the roster of the national amateur team down to twenty men before the deadline imposed by the organizers of the Pan American Games, all without making cuts—his conditioning program would be so rigorous that he would not have to make any.

All the players and coaches moved into the Olympic Stadium, where Avila could watch the players and work them to the bone. He had always emphasized conditioning as a fundamental ingredient for winning teams. Avila's grueling schedule reduced the number of players within two weeks to thirty-five (until then no one had thrown a baseball), and eventually to twenty. No Dominican team had ever before been in such good condition, and none has been since.

When Avila's team got to Panama the players astonished first everyone at the hotel by running up the stairs to their rooms on the seventh floor, then everyone else by asking to play the Cubans in their first game, a bit of psychological warfare that no other team attempted. The Dominicans narrowly lost to Cuba but won every other game, and they went home with a silver medal. From 1980 to 1983 Avila fielded winning teams, beat the Cubans in Caracas at the Pan American Games in 1983, and infused the amateur baseball program with pride.

Each time Avila achieved success or was proved correct in his assessments was a mixed blessing for him. The Dominicans never forgot that he was Cuban-born, or that he was an American working with the Los Angeles Dodgers. But those who admired Avila from afar could not tell that he had become Dominicanized. Avila shifts comfortably from one of his three identities to another depending on the circumstances. This does not reflect opportunism, but rather a desire always to be the outsider: to Americans he is their Latin connection, to Dominicans he represents powerful North American baseball interests, to Cubans he is a turncoat and baseball gadfly.

From the little I saw I discerned two Avilas: the strong, and the circumspect; the taciturn, and the tactful; the gregarious, and the protective. Perhaps his unpredictable nature is his power, his currency, for it enables him to avoid being wedded to Dominican interests and gives him the freedom to criticize them at will. At the same time American interests find him sufficiently Dominican to represent them overseas. Avila embodies the blend of self and other, foreign and local, colonialist and colonial, baseball and politics. Given the strong and somewhat irrational love of baseball in the Caribbean we may yet see Avila "somewhere" in Nicaragua—working for the Dodgers.

5

Yo soy dominicano

Hegemony and Resistance

through Baseball

● ● ● ● ● ● ● ● ●

It is a widely received tenet of cultural imperialism that the cultural exports of the United States and the industrialized West to the rest of the world are uncritically accepted.[1] The baseball institutions and practices of the United States indeed have a powerful influence in the Dominican Republic and other developing countries, as do its other sports and its films, fashions, and television. But it is wrong to assume that the less powerful nations do not possess cultures capable of resisting these influences. In Dominican baseball there are various unique forms of resistance to hegemony and a constant tension between the two forces, either of which will dominate at a given moment depending on the political, economic, and cultural currents.

Hegemony and Cultural Colonialism

"Dominican York" is a slightly derisive term for Dominicans who have moved to New York, become better off economically, and taken to flaunting their newly acquired wealth before their countrymen. They exemplify not only conspicuous consumption and status differentiation among Dominicans, but also the domination of the Dominican Republic by American culture, particularly popular culture. It is characteristic of intercultural relations in the third world that Dominicans should be drawn toward Americans at the same time as they express deep resentment of them. This is in large part due to the control that the United States has over the ideology and consciousness of everyday life

in the Dominican Republic—a control as critical as that of the economic and political kind in maintaining power relations in society and
protecting the position of the United States, as well as that of the dominant Dominican class.

Culture, ideology, and art, once dismissed as a simple reflex of economic systems (that is, as a superstructure bearing a mechanical relation to its base), have been seen to play a more active role by Antonio
Gramsci[2] and Raymond Williams[3] and their followers. Not only coer-
cion (the use of force) but consent (obtained by controlling culture and
consciousness) helps maintain class relations within society and pre-
vents colonies from becoming unstable or even revolutionary. The term
most often applied to cultural and ideological control is hegemony. In
the third world the desire for American culture is often a receding mi-
rage. Many scholars in the rapidly growing field of culture studies have
made this term the cornerstone of their paradigms.[4]

A good deal of confusion surrounds the terms hegemony, resistance,
and economic and political domination. Building on Gramsci, and on
the earlier writings by Marx and Engels in *The German Ideology* that
the class controlling the material means of production also controls the
"mental" means of production,[5] James Scott offers a working definition
of hegemony as "the extent to which dominant classes are able to impose their own vision of a just social order, not only on the behavior of
the subordinate classes, but on their consciousness as well."[6] According
to this definition the dominated class or society accepts the ideology and
cultural institutions of the dominant class or society. Both colony and
colonizer are convinced of the legitimacy of their relationship, the superiority and right of one to dominate the other through a sharing of a
"vision of a just social order." An example is provided by the Dominican Republic, a dominated nation that embraces much of the ideology
and culture of an industrial giant.

The relation between political and economic domination and hegemony is cloudy, especially in a complex society. In both Scott's analysis of a Malaysian village[7] and Genovese's look at slave relations in the
antebellum South,[8] the authors found only a partial or incomplete hegemony. In modern neocolonial relations the nature of hegemony can
be even more elusive, because of the greater number of strata and cultures. Hegemony may work among certain classes more than among
others: for instance, among the affluent class in a third world country it
may be more pronounced than among the poor. Even functioning partially, hegemony nevertheless continues to exert a strong influence.

In partial hegemony the system of domination is flawed: consent by
the dominated is to some extent lacking, and there is a potential for resistance. In discussing why hegemonic control is less perfect among the

Malaysian peasantry than in the industrialized West, Scott points out
that the "institutional bases of hegemony—for example schools and
media—are simply thicker on the ground in late capitalism, and hence
presumably more effective."[9] In Malaysia the cultural distance of the
peasants from the news media and other forms of popular culture allows
more room for their native culture, which they use to resist domination.
But cultural resistance can also occur in the middle of fairly complete
foreign domination in the third world.

Overvaluing the Foreign and Social Self-Loathing

A cause of hegemony that many overlook is ethnic and racial self-loathing. It is the flip side of the desire for the culture of the colonizers. The
dominated party is at least partly convinced of the superiority of the
dominating party, and simultaneously convinced of its own inferiority.
In Scott's otherwise compelling arguments against hegemony, he gives
short shrift to this dimension of hegemony, presumably because its role
in Malaysian class relations is not as great as elsewhere. In most relations between the industrial nations and the third world, however, cultural self-devaluation plays a powerful role.[10]

For people in a nation subject to neocolonialism, the cultural institutions of a country as powerful and wealthy as the United States hold a
special allure, the promise to the colonized of an escape from their dependent status. The colonized consume a wide range of the products of
the colonizers; they subscribe to the ideology of upward mobility and
have the illusion that they can change their status. Thus culture can
promote domination, by offering the promise of empowerment without
change. The desire for the culture and institutions of the foreign elite
(in this case the American elite) rests on two pillars of the social psychology of the dominated: veneration for the foreigner (colonizer, ruling
elite, or multinational corporation) and cultural self-loathing, or what
Fanon referred to as colonial self-hatred.[11] Of course the willingness of a
colonized and subordinate class to take on the ideology and culture of
the ruling class leads to the impoverishment of their own culture.

In writing about his lifelong relationship with the sport of cricket, the
famous black historian C. L. R. James describes how he was often torn
by conflicting loyalties: to the British ideology so embedded in the game
on the one hand, and to Trinidadian values on the other. More effectively and earlier than any other writer, James epitomized the conflicting role of sport in colonialism: "It was only long years after that I
understood the limitation on spirit, vision and self-respect which was
imposed on us by the fact that our master, our curriculum, our code of

morals, everything began from the basis that Britain was the source of all light and leading, and our business was to admire, wonder, imitate, learn; our criterion of success was to have succeeded in approaching that distant ideal—to attain it was of course impossible." [12]

As the Dominicans emulate and consume the culture of the colonizers, they sense they can distance themselves from the feeling of being colonized—it is a balm to them to be able to mimic their oppressors, even if somewhat ineffectively. Not all segments of Dominican society are equally enamored with American culture: its influence is more marked among those with some capacity for upward mobility—the upper and middle classes.

One need look no further than Trujillo for a particularly poignant example of racial and class self-loathing among Dominicans. Trujillo's promotion of Jewish emigration to the Dominican Republic in the 1940s was in part prompted by his hopes that the Jews would "whiten" the Dominican population. Despite having the power of life and death over his people and unbelievable wealth, Trujillo remained very insecure about his darkness, going so far as to lighten his face with powders.

In his political history of the Dominican Republic, Spitzer often notes the Dominican tendency toward simultaneous overvaluation of the foreign and cultural self-devaluation: "It often happened that a Dominican of the upper or middle class would purchase a foreign manufactured good for the prestige value, no doubt to some degree a psychological manifestation of being under [foreign] military rule." [13] Foreign culture gives Dominicans the illusion of upward mobility. The Dominican York weighted down with gold-plated jewelry and the local Dominican wearing a college jersey from an institution in the United States of which he has never heard are giving the same symbolic message: I am becoming less Dominican and more American. The nightly scene at the airport in Santo Domingo bears this out as well. There Dominicans watch their compatriots returning from the United States, who parade the latest in fashion and consumer goods as they leave customs. Even as the locals deride Dominican Yorks for their pretensions, their comments at the airport reveal a desire for the American goods being previewed. Six months later, when these fashions find their way to the Dominican Republic, shoppers will be eager to purchase them.

Political and Economic Domination by the United States

A century of foreign intervention in Dominican economics has done little to improve the country's well-being. While the $735 million in exports that the Dominican Republic made in 1985 represents a significant increase over the levels of the 1970s, it pales by comparison to the $1.5 billion in imports made in the same year. No other country dominates the Dominican Republic as much as the United States does (see chapter 1). Black makes this point in *The Dominican Republic: Politics and Development in an Unsovereign State*, the subtitle of which underscores it: "Because of the overwhelming role of the U.S.-based Gulf and Western Corporation in the Dominican economy since the mid 1960s, the republic has sometimes been called a company state. All major private sectors of the economy—agro-business, mining, tourism, and light manufacturing—are controlled by foreign, mainly U.S., companies."[14]

This represents only the latest phase of an American economic presence dating back to the late nineteenth century.[15] American companies benefited from tax exemptions, and the Dominican government did its part to prevent local competition, assuring American investors that they could get whatever they needed. Trujillo further contributed to the underdevelopment of his country's economy by promoting a single-crop agriculture. The picture was completed by the displacement of peasants and the breakup of communal lands so that American sugar companies (and later Trujillo himself) could expand sugar production.

From the beginning American economic penetration into the Dominican Republic bespoke a corresponding political and cultural domination. As early as the 1870s there was a strong movement to annex the Dominican Republic to the United States, much as Puerto Rico was annexed later.[16] The bid failed to pass in the U.S. Senate by only one vote. Certainly by the beginning of the twentieth century the Dominican government was unable to move in any direction without the approval of the United States.[17]

In the twentieth century the Dominican Republic was twice invaded by the U.S. Marines, and each time the United States had to negotiate an end to armed Dominican resistance, which was particularly fierce during the first invasion (1916–24). Clearly the United States would go to extraordinary lengths to prop up American sugar companies. In the Dominican Republic, as in other third world countries, American companies are largely responsible for the continued underdevelopment.[18] This impoverishment continues to grow despite such schemes as the Caribbean Basin Initiative, allegedly aimed at promoting development. The number of industrial jobs for every hundred urban dwellers actually declined from seven in 1970 to five in 1980.[19] Combined unemployment and underemployment remains around 80 percent, high even by Latin American standards. A century of American presence, planning, and aid has only driven the average Dominican further into despair, as witnessed by the rash of current protests against inflation. The few wealthy families and those who have grown rich and powerful by commandeering wealth that belongs to others have worked hard to keep the interests of the United States in place. Hence: "A revolving door at the upper levels of company and government administration allowed former company managers to serve in important government posts and former government officials to move into company management." [20]

In response to the deprivation in large areas of their country, great numbers of Dominicans seek work and life elsewhere. About one million Dominicans have emigrated to the continental United States and Puerto Rico (the total population of the Dominican Republic is about seven million), most settling in New York and San Juan.

Popular Culture in the Dominican Republic

Dominican popular culture is both indigenous and foreign. Merengue, for instance, a traditional dance and musical form that was formed locally but ultimately stems from African cultural roots, is the dominant form of musical expression and the most widely known indigenous cultural product outside the country. But merengue is not uniform: in response to foreign musical influences, particularly contemporary American music (but also other Latin American music), merengue has become fractured into a number of types, two of which are *típico* (traditional) and *nuevo* (more updated).

Carnival and cockfights are also mass cultural forms in the Dominican Republic, as they are throughout Latin America. While closely tied to religious festivals, the main appeal of Carnival lies in its profaning of the sacred. Throughout Latin America popular festivals such as Carnival have become a rich source of symbols that bond disparate classes and regions into a national whole. Cockfights, on the other hand, appeal almost exclusively to men. In the Dominican Republic attitudes about cockfighting are split. While many see the sport as back-alley barbarism fit only for the common elements, there is a government-sponsored and sanitized version of the sport carried out in a large, well-appointed arena in Santo Domingo. There one finds affluent Dominicans from all walks of society, who are as filled with blood lust as the peasants in the outback and bet as passionately. Cockfighting is intimately linked to the machismo so prevalent in the country and in Latin America, and its appeal cuts across racial and class lines. Because of its peasant roots and its excessive bloodletting the sport has not been picked up by North American interests, and the cockfighting arenas are definitely not among the stops suggested for tourists.

Foreign popular culture, especially from the United States, is as desired as any local form. Almost all film, fashion, and sport is American in origin. All but three movie theaters in Santo Domingo show English-language films exclusively (typically six months after their release in the United States). The genres range from drama and action to comedy and musicals; and whether or not the people understand the premises or subtle points, they attend with alacrity and in large numbers.

Basketball, and of course baseball, are also popular American products,[21] which in the course of being assimilated by Dominicans are often altered. Dominicans can bring their values to bear on the way a game is played, whereas there is little they can do to make foreign television, film, and music distinctly Dominican. For most Dominicans rock music is memorized (even if those who sing it do not know what the words mean), American dance steps are aped, and fashion is slavishly followed.

North American baseball has dominated Dominican versions of the sport. But baseball has also furthered cultural hegemony since early in the twentieth century. In a dispatch sent in 1913 to Secretary of State William Jennings Bryan by James Sullivan, the American minister to the Dominican Republic, the hegemonic potential of the game was openly and seriously suggested:

> I deem it worthy of the Department's notice that the American
> national game of base-ball is being played and supported here
> with great enthusiasm. The remarkable effect of this outlet for the
> animal spirits of the young men, is that they are leaving the
> plazas where they were in the habit of congregating and talking
> revolution and are resorting to the ball fields where they become
> wildly partizan each for his favorite team. The importance of this
> new interest to the young men in a little country like the Domin-
> ican Republic should not be minimized. It satisfies a craving in
> the nature of the people for exciting conflict, and is a real sub-
> stitute for the contest in the hill-sides with rifles, if it could be
> fostered and made important by a league of teams . . . I trust that
> the Department will not believe that this suggestion is a trivial
> one, but will see that it well might be one factor in the salvation
> of the nation.[22]

In contemporary professional baseball, Dominicans experience yet another form of culture that is dominated by the United States. North American major league teams are always in the news, and Dominicans playing in the United States are followed with particular interest by their compatriots. Neighbors and fans hang on every word these successful

Dominicans utter. When they return home Dominican players are often inadvertent spokesmen for American culture. The press reports on everything they say, and players commonly sit in the plazas in the evening and chat about life in the United States as the throngs sit in rapt attention. Each time a Dominican ballplayer succeeds it encourages the efforts of thousands back home to make the supreme effort—to give up education and work toward becoming a baseball player. That successful Dominican ballplayers are so numerous seems to justify any effort to achieve the goal.

Since American baseball teams intensified their involvement with the game at every level in the mid-1970s, Dominican baseball has come to represent a particularly good example of an institution subject to hegemonic control, for the criteria of external domination and consent are both present and the sport is pervasive.

North American popular culture receives much positive attention, and it helps to mediate the more harsh and oppressive forms of domination, both corporate and military. Still, American hegemony is not complete: it is one thing to say that hegemonic influences are at work, and quite another to say that they are overriding. Nations that depend on the industrialized West are entirely capable of stemming foreign cultural domination.

Cultural Resistance

Hegemony and resistance in the Dominican Republic coexist in an unstable, dynamic tension. Culture is the contested terrain, and the Dominican Republic struggles constantly with the United States to control it.

The insights that anthropology provided into culture were its first contribution to the social sciences, and they are still its greatest contribution. Whether materialist or ideological, qualitative or quantitative, oriented toward conflict or toward consensus, anthropological analyses have put cultural factors at the center. Studies of resistance, which have become more widespread in the social sciences, therefore have venerable precursors in cultural anthropology.

Resistance to Western culture can be remarkably persistent, and the form that it takes is varied. It can be religious,[23] psychological,[24] or social.[25] It can be active or passive, overt or covert:

	Active	Passive
Overt	peasant wars slave uprisings	religious sermons that stir up feelings expressions of nationalism

Covert	sabotage	feigned inability to work
	pilfering	songs with hidden meanings

Events and institutions that promote national pride foster cultural resistance by promoting the integrity and cohesiveness of native culture at the expense of foreigners. Since third world culture is often devalued by both foreigners and locals (because of social self-loathing), an act or symbol that promotes local pride is an act or symbol that resists. This theme emerges in Eckstein's anthology on Latin American popular protest.[26] Studies by social scientists of resistance have shown an increased sophistication and subtlety, evidenced in examinations by Scott of ideology and morality as resistance among Malaysian peasants,[27] by Dick Hebdige of the punk subculture in England,[28] and by June Nash of resistance and religion among Bolivian tin miners.[29] (The difference between these works and mine is that they deal with hegemony and resistance within a nation—between classes—whereas my attention is focused on the cultural tension between an industrial power and a developing nation.) In Dominican baseball, resistance is manifested among other ways in the symbolic preferences of the fans, in the way baseball is covered by the press, and in various actions by Dominicans.

About "Culture" in Cultural Resistance

Proponents of the hegemony perspective (such as Williams) sometimes acknowledge that there is resistance to the dominant class ideology and culture (see chapter 7); for this they often use the term "counter hegemony."[30] Their use of the concept is well taken, but the term muddles the issue somewhat, among other things because it suggests that the subordinate group may be achieving dominance over the dominators. A more apt term for the phenomenon of countering hegemony is "cultural resistance."

In some circles there is resistance to the idea of cultural resistance, a skepticism that the contribution of culture to resistance is of much importance. Certainly behavior is the most widely accepted index of overt resistance, especially revolts and acts of sabotage.[31] When acts of resistance shade off into the more subtle realms, it is more difficult to prove the intent of the act. For instance, incompetence on the job may be real, or it may be feigned as part of an organized effort to resist. Similarly, such cultural elements as song, game, film, literature, and folklore have multiple and contradictory levels of meaning. At the manifest level they may appear to uphold the system being resisted, while the at the latent level they may be attacking it. Much good work on this subject has been done on the slavery of the antebellum South. Eugene

Genovese sums up the unique capacities of cultural resistance: "Accommodation itself breathed a critical spirit and disguised subversive actions and often embraced its apparent opposite—resistance."[32]

The work done by historians like Genovese goes far in revealing how servility can be a cover for a host of actions that resist domination. It is culture that is the ammunition in this war. The dominant group uses its culture as an ideological bludgeon, to beat the subordinate class into submission, and sometimes to denigrate the subordinate culture. The subordinate group can appear to be taking on the culture of the dominant group but may in fact be altering it to fit its needs. Hence the struggle is around cultural form and essence: if a subordinate group cannot take on the form while changing the essence, it may simply be acquiescing in its own domination. In any event it should not be assumed that culture is static or exclusively in the hands of the ruling class or society, or that culture is simply a reflection of economic and political forces. It can and does exert its own influence.

In the late 1960s the British social anthropologist Max Gluckman developed a brand of functionalism according to which some acts and symbols that are apparently rebellious will actually defuse socially harmful energy and strengthen society when they are expressed.[33] His term for the expression of these acts and symbols is "ritualized rebellion." Gluckman's formulation represents an advance over earlier functionalism by seeking to explain phenomena that apparently lack function or have conflicting functions. One of the most eloquent adherents of this view, Terry Eagleton, describes the ritualized rebellion of Carnival as "a licensed affair in every sense, a permissible rupture of hegemony, a contained popular blowoff as disturbing and as relatively ineffectual as a revolutionary work of art. As Shakespeare's Olivia remarks, 'There is no slander in an allowed fool.'"[34]

Eagleton and Gluckman read resistance to mean something legitimate and overt, and it is true that "allowed fools" may be limited to propping up the status quo. However, as we know from works by historians on slavery in the antebellum South, slaves too made much of their roles of allowed fools, in the context of the black church[35] and daily life.[36] In their use of the socially sanctioned religious forms of their masters, blacks fashioned a most subtle and powerful form of resistance. This resistance had the potential at times to transform them from allowed fools to practitioners of more threatening forms of resistance. Looked at in this way, all forms of resistance, allowed and illicit, can carry a message that threatens the established order—if not at the moment, then momentarily.

Social scientists have begun to assess the impact of American film and television on ethnic minorities in the United States and abroad.[37]

Their analyses address the issue of hegemony and resistance, at times quite directly. More than twenty-five years ago, however, Herbert Gans argued that the Italian-Americans he studied rejected television that did not reflect their values, while validating television programming that did.[38] His findings implied that the intended messages were comprehended, and that the community shared enough of the dominant culture to determine the acceptability of these messages. Most recently, the anthropologist Christine Gailey has shown that natives of the Pacific island of Tonga interpret American films in terms of their own culture, regardless of the filmmakers' intent.[39] Gailey discusses the novel way in which Tongans interpret the character Rambo as anti-imperialist.

I made several observations along these lines during my stay in the Dominican Republic, and although my evidence is purely anecdotal it supports Gailey's conclusions. At showings of the films *Robocop* and *Platoon*, the reactions of the Dominican audiences were the opposite of what the filmmakers had intended them to be. The message of *Robocop* is clearly one of opposition to corporate strongmen and sympathy for the common folk.[40] But the scenes and dialogue that made North American audiences hiss or laugh at corporate villains only made Dominican audiences applaud. Likewise, scenes from *Platoon*, Oliver Stone's film about American soldiers being killed in Vietnam, were predictably troubling to audiences in the United States, but they were taken lightly by Dominican viewers, some of whom even found them laughable. The response to *Robocop* may reflect in part the Dominicans' ambivalence toward Trujillo. While Dominicans were relieved to be rid of him, they also took to his message of the country's need for strong, centralized leadership. Indeed there are echoes of fascism in the Dominican ideal of The Leader, an all-powerful figure who embodies the national character and plays on the people's hopes and fears.[41] As for the Dominicans' unsympathetic reaction to the dying soldiers of *Platoon*, perhaps in part it reflected their resentment toward the American military. In opposition to works that study the hegemonic potential of American popular culture abroad,[42] Gailey's work shows that cultures have their own agenda and their own issues, and that they can project their values on foreign cultural products. To do this they must have a critical capacity—which some students of hegemony (though by no means all) deny that third world peoples have.

Dominican Resistance: Historical Precedents

The Dominican Republic gives the appearance of complete accommodation to the United States: the government seems compliant, Dominican commerce responds to the dictates of American enterprises both within and outside the country, and people act friendly. But accommodation is not societally uniform: what is subordination at the political and economic level is not necessarily subordination at the cultural level. As Wiarda and Kryzanek point out and as my own observations confirm, there is a resentful and subversive side to Dominicans, which has been borne out in the course of Dominican history.[43]

The depth and extent of the intense Dominican resistance to the occupation by the U.S. Marines in 1916–24 has been painstakingly documented by Bruce Calder, in one of the most impressive pieces of social science research yet written on the Caribbean.[44] In 1920 alone there were 116 incidents of combat reported between guerrillas and U.S. Marines in the eastern part of the country.[45] Hobsbawm's notion of social banditry is particularly appropriate to a discussion of Dominican resistance (social bandits are outlaws according to those in power, marginally organized and politically oriented), since it was as "bandits" (*gavilleros*) that these displaced peasants were referred to by the American administrators in the area. The military resistance waged by the insurgents lasted five and a half years (1917–22), during which there were roughly 370 military contacts between guerrillas and American troops. Although there were relatively few casualties, the Dominican peasants succeeded in tying up the Marines. At first the American military governor wrote off the insurgents, but the organized caudillos received so much support from other peasants that their military effectiveness as well as the organized structure of their resistance had to be acknowledged.

The eastern guerrilla campaign dovetailed with the rise of nationalism in the urban centers, but there was virtually no formal link between the insurgents in the east and the intellectual and political leaders in Santo Domingo and other cities. Calder cites as explanations the traditionalism of the elite class and regional disdain in the west for the feudalistic caudillos and their ragtag peasant retainers.[46] But by making use of the bandstand and of the press, which at the time was heavily censored, the nationalists mobilized national opinion against the outrages committed almost daily by the Americans. They strove to make contacts with other Caribbean leaders and eventually with influential American politicians and the American Federation of Labor.

It is important that culture was the currency of the nationalists' campaign, and that the Dominican elite debated furiously over the role of North American culture (as they continue to do periodically). Some felt that taking on the cultural traits of the foreign power was justified if it led to progress; others felt that doing so was tantamount to "yanquization" and servility, that those who slavishly imitated the culture of the United States and sought to consume their way to being American were "more imperialistic than the imperialists."[47] As the nationalists worked to heighten the outrage of their countrymen over the increasing racism and oppressiveness of the United States, they promoted native culture in all areas of life. It was during this period that the merengue became the national dance and musical form, the boy scouts were formed, and baseball became the national game.[48] It was also during the American military occupation that nationalists brought literary works and poetry to the national consciousness.[49] Whereas the guerrillas met the Americans with force, the nationalists confronted them with legal, political, and ideological maneuvering. Their ideological and cultural campaign was always punctuated by large rallies and protests when some outrage perpetrated by the United States was made known.[50]

Four decades later a military coup deposed President Juan Bosch (1963), rival political parties took to the streets, and the U.S. Marines again intervened in the Dominican Republic (1965–66). Several thousand Dominicans lost their lives in the turmoil that followed. With the memories of the earlier occupation still fresh in the minds of older Dominicans and a part of national folklore, it took little time for Dominicans to resist both physically and emotionally. Another wave of poets, artists, and authors villainized the gringos and lionized the Dominican nationalists. The effects of this second invasion continue to be felt by many middle-aged and older Dominicans.

Dominican Baseball as Resistance

Cultural resistance has been documented in sport. The ethnographic film *Trobriand Cricket* dramatically depicts how inhabitants of the Trobriand Islands in Papua New Guinea mold the sport of the colonizers, cricket, to reflect their cultural needs. Other studies (discussed below) show how baseball has been similarly used in other cultures.

On the surface the case for Dominican resistance in baseball seems weak, given the degree of domination by the United States and the stifling presence of American major league franchises and scouts. The dark years of the occupation by the U.S. Marines of their country gave the Dominicans little to be happy about. Baseball was one of the bright spots, however. There were games played between U.S. Marines and Dominican clubs, and while young Fellicita Guerra refused to be on the same diamond with these foreign invaders, others preferred to fight the marines by any means available. American periodicals published in Santo Domingo for the forces but read by Dominicans declared that in the games between North Americans and Dominicans "the Marines

have to be champions by virtue of their ethnic and intellectual superiority and because Dominicans can be champions of nothing."[51] This
infuriated Dominicans but also filled the city with interest in the forthcoming match between Licey and the Marines. Francisco Rodríguez,
nineteen years old, became immortalized when he hit a home run with
the bases empty as his team was losing 2 to 1 in the ninth inning with
two men out. The Licey club was so filled with pride and resentment
that it held the yanquis scoreless in the tenth inning before scoring the
winning run. Such victories were like a balm for battered Dominicans
and were by no means treated as entertaining and meaningless. They
provided hope and vindication, as well as cherished memories to be
passed on to succeeding generations.

Dominicans have been so successful at the game that they sense they
are in charge of it, that they are at least the equals of the North Americans. The Dominicans have shown how a form of foreign popular culture can be used to resist hegemonic influences; and, at least sym-
bolically, they have contradicted the notion that economic domination
automatically results in cultural domination and cultural inferiority.

During the season of 1987–88 I attended games at Estadio Quisqueya, an impressive stadium with almost sixteen thousand seats that is
home to both professional teams in Santo Domingo. Apart from some
Spanish billboards, the stadium is indistinguishable from a minor
league stadium in North America. The great difference lies in the spectators and their cultural behavior (see chapter 6).

At the ballpark one night I concentrated on people wearing T-shirts
and hats bearing the insignia not only of Dominican professional teams
but of American major league teams. People are symbolic animals who
assign meaning to most things. A symbol can be sacred, like a clan
totem or crucifix, or charged with great secular meaning, like the Con-
gressional Medal of Honor, or mundane, like the paintings in the tee-
pees of the Plains Indians, the safety pins of punks, or the colors that
people wear on the street. Because Dominican fans use color not only
to identify with a team but also as a sign of their political affiliation, I
thought that by examining the insignia worn at ballgames I could com-
pile a rough but valid index of identification with national resistance on
the one hand and American hegemony on the other. I decided to ask
those who chose Dominican symbols why they did so. I designed a
questionnaire with seven items (see Appendix) and conducted a survey
during three night games at Estadio Quisqueya, and at two sites one
afternoon outside the stadium (one in a poor neighborhood, the other
in an affluent one). My assistant and I interviewed 190 people chosen at
random, which yielded 164 responses that were complete and usable

(n = 164). While the sample is small, the results are highly patterned and suggest conclusions that are worthy of further exploration.

My initial working assumption was that hegemony rather than resistance would prevail, that Dominicans would follow their general patterns of cultural consumption and choose an American baseball cap rather than one of a local Dominican team (cost, availability, and quality being equal). The results were surprising: only 22 percent (36 of 164) chose an American cap, 78 percent (128 of 164) a Dominican one.

The reasons the fans gave for their selections quickly explained these unexpected results. These reasons were unambiguously and strongly nationalist and moreover were overwhelmingly framed in positive rather than anti-American terms. Among heavily colonized people nationalism is usually weak, and where it is pronounced it tends to be accompanied by hostility toward foreigners. The following were typical of the fans' statements about their selections and their feelings of national pride:

> [Respondent 4:] Yo soy dominicano! I'm Dominican! This is my country, so I go for the Licey [name of local team].

> [Respondent 32:] Tradition! The best thing in the world is to be a Liceyista!

> [Respondent 42:] Escogido is the team of my country.

> [Respondent 12:] I'm a nationalist. Of course I go for Licey!

For some fans the choice was more difficult. They would name as their favorite American teams those with a record of having signed Dominican players (Toronto, Los Angeles, Pittsburgh), but would have trouble deciding between an American symbol and a Dominican one. When pressed they generally opted for the cap of a local team:

> [Respondent 99:] I'm a Cibaeño [from the Cibao region of the country]. Toronto has a lot of Dominicans but I'm a Cibaeño first.

> [Respondent 122:] I like L.A. because they help Licey, but the team of my birthplace is Licey. I'm a Liceyista.

> [Respondent 63:] Even though some Dominicans are [in the United States] and we follow the game in the U.S., it's not the same. It's our baseball here.

It is noteworthy that many of the respondents who chose a Dominican symbol (perhaps most) made clear that they interpreted the hat as a symbol of their nation. Those who favored an American cap, however, typically gave a reason related to baseball:

[Respondent 19:] Escogido is the team of my country, but the Dodgers are a higher-quality team.

[Respondent 144:] [The Toronto Blue Jays] play the real baseball. Here we just follow them.

It was surprising that only four of the 164 respondents adopted an anti-American tone, particularly because at the time of the survey Dominican demonstrators were accusing the Americans of having wrecked their economy. These were some typical negative statements:

[Respondent 77:] I'm Dominican! I'm not *some gringo* who wears a Dodger hat!

[Respondent 100:] Everybody likes foreign things. But if we follow that we'll be in a big hole in the sea.

Although my working assumption was disproved, there was a second hypothesis that would be consistent with the results I obtained: upper-class Dominicans might associate more strongly than poorer Dominicans with things American. This would be consistent with my observations and with most hegemonic analyses of imperialism.

At first I separated Dominicans by class, by assuming that those sitting in box seats were more affluent than those sitting in reserved seats and bleachers.[52] This assumption turned out to be misleading, since for various reasons many affluent people sit in the cheaper seats (for one thing they are closer to the bookies who congregate in the upper reaches of the stadium). I then decided to distinguish class according to occupation, a technique employed by Weil, Black, and Blutstein[53] and by Wiarda and Kryzanek,[54] and found that class was a predictor of whether a Dominican or an American cap would be chosen: the 83 respondents who held professional, entrepreneurial, middle-management, and civil service jobs chose the Dominican cap by a margin of 58 to 25 (70 percent to 30 percent), while the 81 respondents who were clerks, laborers, and shopkeepers chose the Dominican cap by a margin of 70 to 11 (86 percent to 14 percent).

The preferences of fans provide evidence of both resistance and hegemony. What is unique and surprising is that the pattern of Dominican preference for North American cultural artifacts should be broken in the realm of baseball, the prototypical sport of the North Americans. Baseball is in effect the Dominican vehicle for resistance to American cultural domination, and this is no accident (see below). It is also noteworthy that class is an important variable in the preferences of fans: the upper class identifies far more readily with the symbols of the North

Americans, just as the lower class is more apt to support left-leaning candidates like Juan Bosch.

Resistance in the Press

The print media offer a more kaleidoscopic view of passive and active Dominican resistance than do the electronic media, the impact of which is limited by poverty and nationwide power blackouts. Dominican print journalists are also more sophisticated and better informed than local television journalists.

Reporters admit that they try to sell newspapers by appealing to public emotion, but they also try to retain respectability. As I followed the coverage of baseball between 1987 and 1989 in Santo Domingo's leading daily paper, *Listin diario*, I noted among other things this tendency to emphasize emotionally loaded subjects and play to popularly held views. This ulterior motive notwithstanding, the Dominican baseball press has also developed a reporting style that fosters nationalism as cultural resistance—though it has not done so altogether consciously.

One of the first things that struck me about the way the Dominican press covered general news was that there was little outrage directed against North America in the front pages, even though the country was battered by a serious economic crisis that was caused at least in part by the policies of the United States. Headlines and stories noted the difficult conditions, but fingers rarely pointed north.

When covering baseball, on the other hand, the papers were willing to blame problems on North American major league teams. Again one is moved to ask why this is true of baseball but not of politics and economics.

Whether the Dominican press is covering baseball, tennis, or basketball, North American domination is made very clear. The United States has the biggest contests, the most money, and the most glamour. This is surely the way baseball is covered by the North American press, which is markedly ethnocentric.[55] "Foreign" baseball is treated by the North American press as unusual, even quaint. Japanese baseball, for instance, is usually the object of polite condescension.[56] American players in Japan are reported on only occasionally, in general when they are doing so well that they may attempt to reenter the American major leagues. For example, on 16 April 1988 the *New York Times* relegated the news that the former Yankee pitcher Bill Gullickson was playing in Japan to a short paragraph buried in the back of the sports section. An article in *Sports Illustrated* on Bob Horner commented: "American import Bob Horner made a smashing debut in Japan: six games, six hom-

ers."[57] This was followed by an article on Randy Bass, another American playing brilliantly in Japan and harboring a desire to return home.
The implication was that if a ballplayer were any good at all he would
be playing in the United States. Cecil Fielder's impressive reentry into
the major leagues in 1990 after playing in Japan may mark a change in
direction, since Japan seems more able than ever before to tap into the
free-agent market; but it is more likely that Fielder is the exception that
proves the rule. By contrast, the Dominican press sees the possibility
that a Dominican might play in Japan as much more important, and
gives the news more prominence.[58] Baseball coverage in the Dominican
Republic reflects the mixed feelings of the Dominican people: pride in
the accomplishments of Dominican players from the 1960s onward and
a growing acknowledgement that the country has won a special place in
the world of baseball are tempered by the view that Dominican baseball
is still an adjunct to the American game. Dominican baseball writers
bow to American domination, yet at the same time they are defiant and
nationalistic, touting the accomplishments of Dominicans and sniping
at the United States.

The biggest story in baseball in early 1988 was the record set by the
Baltimore Orioles when they lost their first twenty-one games. Newspapers in all countries interested in baseball covered the streak, and on
the day the Orioles finally won *Listin diario* declared in bold headlines:
"Baltimore Breaks Losing Chain." In the preceding weeks the paper had
painted daily pictures of dejection and hope, and noted among other
things that some residents of Baltimore had sought the help of sorcerers
to break the spell (this aroused a lot of interest in the Dominican Republic, where voodoo remains influential). But the story of the Orioles
was the exception: all the other headlines and stories in the Dominican
press in April 1988 were of Dominican baseball exploits. Were one to
judge major league baseball from the press coverage in Santo Domingo,
one would assume that most baseball players were Dominican, or at
least that most of the best players were. Whether covering the North
American major leagues in the summer or the Dominican league in the
winter, the Dominican press is highly nationalistic.

One is immediately struck by the sheer number of lead stories about
Dominican players, especially during the season of the Dominican Professional Baseball League. The stories can recount the outcome of
league games ("[Licey] Tigers Beat Eastern Stars, Pass to Finals"), or the
latest turn of events in the contract negotiations of Dominicans playing
in the major leagues ("Pirates Contract for Rafael Belliard"), or some
Dominican crisis ("Griffin Thinks That D.R. Baseball Will Recover Its
Force"). Articles on North Americans and North American subjects are
scarce during the winter season. They tend to focus on the unusual and

outstanding (such as the record salary Orel Hershiser got from the Los Angeles Dodgers), on non-Dominican Hispanic players (from other Latin American countries such as Puerto Rico, Mexico, and Venezuela), and on North American players of Hispanic origin (such as Jose Canseco and Keith Hernandez).

Summer Reporting: Dominicans Abroad

During the summer the focus is on the United States, where Dominican players are closely followed. The lead story in a paper published in Santo Domingo may be about a Dominican scheduled to pitch ("De León and Pérez Scheduled to Pitch Games Today," or "Today Pascual Pérez Looks for Expo Victory Record"), or about the games played the previous day ("Bell, Guerrero and Liriano Homer; Rijo Wins"). Only when there is a major breakthrough or record does the lead story have a non-Dominican topic (such as the losing streak of the Baltimore Orioles).

Summer box scores and game reports are usually on the second page of the sports section. A headline the width of the page will have accounts of all of the day's action beneath it, and each article about a game has its own, smaller headline in boldface. These headlines prove very revealing. One issue of *Listin diario* included the following primary and secondary headlines:

Main headline: Bell, Guerrero and Liriano Homer; Rijo Wins
Smaller headlines: 1. [Story without headline, on game between Toronto Blue Jays and Minnesota Twins]
2. Tigers 11, Royals 4
3. Samuel 0 for 4
4. Seattle Wins
5. Franco 3 for 6
6. Guante Pitches
7. Guerrero 3 for 4; Griffin 3 for 4
8. Uribe 2 for 3
9. Rijo Wins; Ramírez 2 for 4; Garcia 0 for 1 [59]

The main headline is notable in that it mentions three players, each from a different team, who have in common only their Dominican nationality. Some of the smaller headlines summarize the outcome of a game; others summarize the performance of an individual player (in all cases a Dominican), and the outcome of the game is secondary. Between 5 April and 2 May 1988 I recorded the main headline on the second page of twenty-two issues of *Listin diario*, and counted the number of secondary headlines that referred to the performance of an individual player (as well as the total number of secondary headlines):

5 April Uribe 2 for 3; Soto No Decision	1 of 5
8 April Peña Wins First; Guerrero Decides It	3 of 6
10 April Bell, Guerrero, and Liriano Homer	7 of 9
12 April Samuel Strokes Two Hits	4 of 4
13 April José De León Wins First Game	4 of 6
14 April Fernández Hits 2 for 4; Samuel Gets a Hit	6 of 7
15 April Camposano Slaps First Home Run	2 of 8
16 April José Rijo Wins; Samuel Tows Two	3 of 6
17 April Pedro Guerrero 3 for 4, 4 RBIs	6 of 9
18 April García Decides for Atlanta; Pérez Wins	5 of 9
19 April Santana Connects for H.R., Double, Single	3 of 5
20 April Bell, Lee, and Peña All Strike 2 Singles	5 of 8
21 April Baltimore Breaks Record for Most Losses	4 of 7
22 April Tony Peña Strokes Two Home Runs	3 of 5
23 April Belliard Triple; Cuta and De León Lose	6 of 8
24 April Alfredo Griffin Slaps Triple and Single	3 of 4
25 April Fernández Connects HR; Belliard a Triple	8 of 13
27 April Baltimore Loses 19th in Row	3 of 6
28 April Cuta Wins over Soto; Balt. Loses 20th	3 of 6
30 April Baltimore Breaks Losing Streak	0 of 4
1 May Samuel Smashes Triple; Drives In 3	3 of 3
2 May Melido Pérez Wins 2d; Javier 3 for 5	6 of 10
Total	88 of 148

Nineteen of the twenty-two main headlines dealt with the accomplishments of an individual player rather than the outcome of a game, as did 64 percent of the secondary headlines. If the outcome of a game was the subject of a headline it was usually because there were no Dominicans or Latinos playing, a fact noted in the story. For instance, on 1 May *Listin diario* printed the headline "Brewers Win" above a story that noted: "Latinos did not participate in this encounter." In the same issue it was noted that "no Latinos play for Boston."

In contrast to accounts of games in North American papers, which seldom make any mention of a player's nationality, those in Dominican papers prominently note the nationalities of key Hispanic players and stars, as in the following description in *Listin diario* of a game between Toronto and Minnesota: "For Minnesota the Panamanian Juan Berenguer pitched one and two-thirds innings, permitted two hits, struck out four, and walked one. For Toronto the Dominican Tony Fernandez was 1 for 5, his countryman George Bell was 2 for 4, the Puerto Rican Juan Beníquez added a run in two turns at bat, the other Quisqueyena [a colloquialism for Dominican] Manny Lee hit a single in three trips and scored a run while his compatriot Nelson Liriano went 1 for 4."[60]

The highly favorable comparison of Latinos to non-Latinos is for the most part implicit but constant. In its report of a game played on 20 April between the Toronto Blue Jays and the Kansas City Royals, in which the Blue Jay players Ernie Whitt, Fred McGriff, and Jesse Barfield (all Americans) combined for six hits and ten runs batted in, *Listin diario* focused instead on the performance of Bell (one run batted in) and Lee (two singles). In general the press treated Bell's performance as the key to the win, and used it as a pretext for citing his impressive showing on opening day (which it had already played up incessantly): "Dominican George Bell, who pegged three home runs against Saberhagen in the opening day of the season, pushed across one run with a single."[61]

In a game on 25 April Tony Fernández hit a home run for Toronto; *Listin diario* made this the subject of its main headline ("Fernández Connects for Home Run"), while the *Toronto Globe and Mail* put it in the context of the game results and the *New York Times* mentioned it only in passing ("and Kelly Gruber and Tony Fernández each hitting one [home run] in the third"). Dominicans have taken it on themselves to make heroes of their players one and all, and to a lesser extent of other Latinos. Clearly, the trumpeting of Dominican accomplishments comes at the expense of North Americans, who are the victims of invidious comparisons.

The special slant it gives to daily coverage is only one tool that the press has in fostering cultural resistance. In addition to the routine daily coverage and box scores there are special summer stories devoted to specific players and issues. There seem to be four types: special interest stories on individual players, and stories about honors won and standards set by Dominican players, wealth gained by Dominicans (usually in contract negotiations), and crises in baseball.

Except perhaps in Cuba, where the cult of personality is ideologically disdained as a product of bourgeois society, stories that highlight individual athletes are integral to sports journalism. Sportswriters make athletes into folk heroes by putting then at the center of their stories and exaggerating their accomplishments. The treatment is the same whether the player is a legitimate star like Roger Clemens, a local favorite like José Rijo, or a mere journeyman. But the more mediocre the athlete, the more likely it is that the journalist will focus on some aspect of the athlete's private life or personality (this sort of reporting has become known as "up close and personal"). American culture is strongly individualistic, and the American fascination with celebrity and popular psychology has reached gargantuan proportions. This has had both bad and

good results: the triviality of magazines like *People* and television shows
like "Lifestyles of the Rich and Famous" on the one hand, and a surprisingly strong interest in serious books like Christopher Lasch's *The
Culture of Narcissism* on the other.[62] Sportswriters also reflect this polar-
ity. There is no shortage of unimaginative and incompetent baseball
writers, but there are also those like Roger Angell of the *New Yorker* and
Thomas Boswell of the *Washington Post* who transcend convention.

Athletes who are larger than life, like Hershiser and Bell, pose their
own problems. Once stories of their heroic accomplishments on the
field have been written and rewritten, the journalist must satisfy the rapidly growing demands of their fans by finding something else to write
about. This is where Dominican baseball writers part company with
North American writers, for they lack the tradition of writing about athletes' life off the field. Dominican journalists are also less well trained
than their American counterparts (there are no schools of journalism in
the Dominican Republic), and they tend to repeat the same information again and again. They often get their stories secondhand. A typical
article makes one point from which the writer deviates little, and is extremely short (even by comparison with the shorter articles in North
American papers). It is rare for a Dominican sports story to be more
than five hundred words long; most are about two to three hundred
words long. But what the writers lack in depth they make up for in the
frequency with which they write similar stories about their baseball heroes. Perhaps this is because they limit their range and write almost exclusively about Dominican professional players in the United States, in
contrast to reporters in the United States, who generally cover a variety
of sports in their own metropolitan area, in addition to providing personal angles on the players. The result is the same: both types of reporting have the effect of building legends and making baseball omnipresent. Hence any single first page of a sports section is likely to include (in
addition to other sports stories) bold headlines about Bell, Guerrero,
and Pascual Pérez, each of whom plays for a different team. These are
at times supplemented by three-color sketches or photographs of the
players. The effect of this coverage is the same as in the United States: to
elevate the player to heroic proportions.

Kudos and Honors

During the winter of 1987–88 the Dominican press (like the North
American press) was full of stories about Bell, the outfielder for the
Toronto Blue Jays who had been voted the American League's Most
Valuable Player for 1987. (This award is the most coveted in baseball,

but there are many smaller awards and honors that fuel the Dominican nationalist train. For instance, *Listin diario* once declared in bold headlines: "Pedro Guerrero Is Elected the Latin Player of the Week.")[63] Bell's performance in the first week of the season in 1988 set the tone for the press for the entire summer. On 10 April *Listin diario* ran a huge headline that read: "Uncontainable George Bell Is Elected A.L. Best of the Week." The appetite of all Dominican fans was whetted by the article beneath, which treated three North American players as also-rans: "George Bell of the Toronto Blue Jays, who introduced a major league record with three home runs in the opening game, was named American League player of the week in the first week of the season. Bell, the Most Valuable Player of the American League last year, batted .455 and had four round-trippers for the week. Others named were Pete O'Brien of Texas, Dave Winfield of New York, and Cory Snyder of Cleveland."

Many Dominican fans are beginning to expect their players to perform consistently at this high level. They get a feeling of superiority as they read about Dominican players winning awards and piling up impressive statistics. One page-long article in *Ultima hora* was fairly typical of what they read: "With the first two months of the 1987 season coming to a conclusion this weekend, the acts of more or less twelve Latin American players were listed among the top one hundred with the best statistics in the twenty-four teams [of major league baseball]. In this group the likelihood of the Dominicans Pedro Guerrero of the Los Angeles Dodgers, and George Bell of the Toronto Blue Jays, and of the Venezuelan Andrés Galarraga to predominate from the first eight weeks to the end of the season seems certain."[64]

These kinds of predictions and statistical comparisons are as regular a feature in the Dominican press as they are in the American press. What is distinctive about Dominican coverage is its nationalistic bent, which feeds cultural and national pride and reduces the need felt by the readers to prove themselves against *los blancos* (the whites), to gain the approval of the North Americans.

The Dominican papers not only list the major league leaders in all the usual categories but keep a separate set of statistics for Latinos:

> The Latin American Department of United Press International today elected Dominican Pedro Guerrero of the Los Angeles Dodgers as the most outstanding Latino in major league baseball for the week of April 11 to 17.[65]

> The Dominican Republic has newly demonstrated its reputation of being a quarry of baseball players in the production of the most players nominated for the all-Hispanic major league team . . . Of

the nineteen players selected by six baseball writers that were interviewed by phone, eight are Dominican. Seven of the Dominicans live in the city of San Pedro de Macorís. The rest are
composed of six Puerto Ricans, two Mexicans, one Venezuelan,
and one Nicaraguan . . . Norm Clark, baseball writer of the
paper the *Rocky Mountain News* of Denver Colorado, said that
the all-star list of Hispanic outfielders "ends with Bell . . . I feel
that he could be the newly named Most Valuable Player this
year," said Clark.[66]

Having set apart the athletic accomplishments of Latinos from those
of North Americans, the Dominican writers often compare one Latino
with another. One headline asked: "Guerrero or Bell; Who Is Better?"
The article seemed to take for granted that the two were better than
everyone else: "With the rise to the big leagues of José Joaquín Bautista,
the total is 111 Dominican players since Osvaldo Virgil arrived in 1956.
Actually we have around thirty-five players in the big leagues, among
them George Bell and Pedro Guerrero. There are no doubts that thousands of fans ask, 'Who is better, Bell or Guerrero?' Bell and Guerrero
are of the players that since they arrived home all the world waits for
their home runs."[67] Having defined categories of Latino baseball statistics and honors, the press has inadvertently created a Latino universe of
discourse, one in which North Americans are conspicuously absent.

Reporting Player Salaries

Reports of contract negotiations generally center on the large sums involved rather than the details. Read over a period of time, the headlines
seem as regular as the tide. They inspire thousands of young players
who hope for a similar offer someday:

> Rufino Receives Offers from Various Countries
> Fernández Signs for Five Million Dollars
> Guzmán Signs with the Texas Rangers

At times the salaries of all Dominican players in the major leagues
are added up, and the total is treated as if it were a major cultural
achievement. The headline on the front page of *Listin diario* on 4 April
1988 read: "Dominicans in the Big Leagues Earn $15,454,880 U.S."
The article beneath the headline gave the salary of each of the thirty-
five Dominican major leaguers. The message has a meaning in the Dominican Republic that is different from what it would be in the United

States: to the Dominicans baseball is less a game than a way of escaping poverty and building national pride. The salaries of the players stimulate national interest in the game, as does the accessibility of the players (some go to the ballparks to help the amateurs). As one fan put it, the enormous salaries are "a cultural treasure. It is proof that we are great." Much as archeological treasures attest to a rich Dominican past, salaries attest to the present.

Winter Baseball Coverage: Crises in Dominican Baseball

The uncertain health of Dominican baseball is of paramount concern in the Dominican Republic. The most pressing issues in the past few years have been a decline in the number of Dominican players who return home, the concomitant weakening of the league, a decline in attendance, the premature departure from the Dominican league of North American players, and the tendency of major league teams to dictate to Dominican players whether and how much they can play in their native country. In all these areas the press has attributed the problem to interference by American interests.

Falling attendance was without any doubt the big issue of the Dominican baseball season of 1988–89. Many explanations were given in the press, of which the most frequently cited was the economic bind the country was in. Inflation was raising the price of everything: tickets for the games, transportation to and from the games, and even food at the ballparks. The owner of the Aguilas of the Cibao, one of the oldest and most well established clubs in the Dominican Republic, became exasperated when he took a huge loss at the end of the season: "'It was a true disaster,' Ricardo Tito Hernández, president of the Aguilas Cibaenas, said yesterday . . . He understands that winter baseball is going very badly because the fans have been keeping their distance from the stadiums. Hernández is pessimistic about the future of paid baseball if they don't find some economic stability in the country."[68]

Another reason given for the flagging attendance was the refusal of Dominican athletes to play in their homeland once they had earned large salaries in the United States. But the Dominican press did not blame the players; it was rather the owners and indirectly the Americans who were taken to task for the high salaries paid to imported North American players: "On the other hand, as for the number of native big league ballplayers that do not want to play here because of the lack of an adequate salary and security, I have the solution: give it all to them, and don't bring 'importados.'"[69] By scapegoating the North Americans the

Dominican press can heighten the emotions of its readers, claim credit

for fixing blame, and keep North America at a distance. This distancing
is perhaps the most potent form of cultural resistance.

At no time is the distance greater than when North American teams
tamper with Dominican professional teams. While major league franchises have been enmeshed in the internal affairs of Dominican teams
for many decades, tampering is a more recent development. Several instances of tampering came to the attention of the press and fans in the
winter season of 1988–89. The first involved Rafael Ramírez, who allegedly was prevented by the Houston Astros, to whom he was under
contract, from playing for his Dominican team, the Estrellas Orientales. At least one well-placed official argued that Ramírez did not really
want to play and was only being urged on by the the people of San
Pedro de Macorís. The official also said that after a few games with the
Estrellas Orientales, Ramírez became involved in negotiations with the
Astros—and that Ramírez used the Astros' purported desire that he not
play with the Estrellas Orientales as a pretext for quitting. According to
this source Ramírez's decision was motivated by a reluctance to jeopar-
dize a lucrative new contract. The press, on the other hand, fanned the
flames by interpreting the issue in nationalist terms: "The general manager of the Estrellas Orientales yesterday asked for the expulsion of the
Houston Astros representatives in this country for the attitude assumed
by that organization to prevent the Dominican Rafael Ramírez from
playing with the Macorís club . . . 'We can never, under any criteria,
accept an organization affecting our national sport in such a way as to
impede a title to the people [of San Pedro de Macorís].'" [70] Whether or
not the general manager was being completely frank, it was revealing
that he chose to come out so aggressively against the American club,
and that he did so on nationalist grounds.

A second case of tampering involved José Rijo, who plays for the Cincinnati Reds in the United States and the Licey team at home. His allegations against the Reds, similar to those that Ramírez had made against
the Astros, came as he was embroiled in a contract dispute with the
Reds and as Licey was playing in the Championship Series. The incident surrounding Rijo provoked even more controversy than that surrounding Ramírez: "The Cincinnati Reds yesterday prohibited the Dominican pitcher José Rijo, currently a reliever from pitching in the final
series that began last night . . . The same pitcher offered the information and explained that the manager of the Reds expressed to him that
he could pitch one or two times, but not daily and not hard . . . 'I want
to pitch but it's not my decision. They want me to remain healthy for
spring training' he said." [71]

To me Rijo reiterated his relative powerlessness in the face of the dictates of his American employers. When I asked him whether the Reds could really stop him from playing he replied: "They do! . . . they told me not to pitch two days in a row. I came here and pitched four days in a row. Now they call me back and they're mad at me. They cannot stop me, but I don't want them mad at me. They are a priority for me. Here, you get ready, work on some pitch, for going back there." [72]

By declaring his powerlessness and placing the blame on the Cincinnati Reds, Rijo confirmed that the American major leagues are dominant and the Dominican league subordinate, that Dominican baseball is a training ground for the Americans. This inequality is however denied by the Dominican press, which engages in an overt form of cultural resistance by viewing the Dominican league not as a subordinate but as a sovereign entity that has been slighted.

Another way American teams interfere with Dominican baseball is by having North Americans who play in the Dominican Republic leave before the season is over. This too causes outrage, because while the Dominicans do not always feel positively toward the *importados* the Dominican owners do depend on them, especially in the stretch drive toward the championship. This was dramatically portrayed as the Escogido Lions began the Championship Series in 1988. With his contract valid only until 23 January, the Detroit Tigers refused to extend the stay of their player Mark Huisman for another week, saying that he had to get ready for spring training in the United States. The article that appeared that same day, which spoke of Huisman as a "gentleman and an athlete," was belied by the headline, which screamed, "Bomber Huisman Abandons the Lions." In the body of the article the Detroit Tigers were implicated by Daniel Aquino, the president of the Escogido Lions: "Aquino, in his declarations, revealed that the directive of the Detroit Tigers, with whom the standout reliever is affiliated, asked him to report three weeks before Spring Training." [73]

Some of the Americans stayed for the Championship Series, contributing to the victory of Escogido. But as the team prepared to go to Mexico for the Caribbean Series, the Americans, who accounted for most of the pitching staff, announced that they would not be going along. This desertion was especially painful in the light of Huisman's recent departure, and it prompted a steady stream of anti-American invective in the press. For all their grudging acceptance of foreigners on Dominican teams, the papers bellowed the following morning, "Lions Importados Will Not Go to Series." The articles noted the presumed need of the players to "rush" back to the United States for spring training, yet the accompanying photographs showed the Americans lounging about, half dressed, in the offices of the Escogido Lions. This gave the impression

that there was really no hurry to return after all and implied that the Dominicans were being deceived.

Next to an article about Huisman was another taking to task the American manager of a Dominican team for having lost so badly in the championship series. Cultural differences were cited as the major stumbling block: "not knowing how to handle Latin players" was the way both the paper and various people phrased it. Another American managed a rival team with much better results, and the press treated him more favorably because he knew how to handle the players. This manager, like Lasorda, has the respect of the Dominicans because of his willingness to return regularly to the Dominican Republic. Few North Americans realize that their attitudes toward the Dominicans are a subject that the Dominicans are very sensitive about, and few are aware of the acrimonious history between the two cultures.

Summer reporting of baseball and winter reporting are different on the surface but similar beneath it. In the summer Dominicans are depicted as stellar athletes capable of competing at the highest level. This brand of reporting exemplifies positive cultural resistance; its subtext is that the North Americans are not invincible and that the Dominicans have a way of dominating them in the United States. During the winter, when the major league teams and their Dominican stars are no longer playing, cultural resistance takes a negative form: the emphasis is on the crisis in Dominican baseball, which the North Americans are seen as having brought on. Both the positive cultural resistance of the summer and the negative cultural resistance of the winter are effective in molding public opinion and in putting distance between Dominican culture and American culture.

Concrete Resistance

When I began studying Dominican baseball I expected to find more acts of resistance among players in the academies, who are novices, and fewer among more experienced players who had been socialized into the culture of professional North American baseball. My thinking was that resistance would be inversely correlated to dependency.

For two years I agonized over my inability to find what I considered acts of cultural resistance: organized patterns of behavior, subtle or not, that held foreign influences at bay. At the academies I would see boys whose behavior posed problems, but these were not patterned responses (see chapter 4). My frustration ended one day when I watched a group of young men trying out for the academy and suddenly realized why organized, patterned resistance could never occur there: these boys wanted only to comply. I had been looking for resistance in the wrong place.

It then occurred to me that resistance is born of a conflict between disparate cultural elements: it was only after they had tasted the bittersweet fruit of success in North America and returned to their homeland that the boys could begin to resist, that someone like Fellicita Guerra could refuse a rare chance to play in North America because of his opposition to the occupation by the U.S. Marines of his homeland in 1920 (see chapter 1), or that Chico Contón could abandon his pursuit of baseball in the United States because of the racism he encountered— obviously an act of refusal, though one given less attention than Guerra's (see chapter 3). Once I had realized this I decided to look anew at the Dominican winter league.

The Fight for Free Agency and FENAPEPRO

The move toward greater assertiveness by FENAPEPRO in 1988–89 was prompted by the unpopular proposal of Monchín Pichardo at the beginning of the season that the Dominican league should take a "rest" (see chapter 3). Under its current president the organization has waged an uphill battle for free agency that recalls the one that was played out in the United States in the 1970s. To succeed FENAPEPRO needs better organization than it has. The owners may try to oppose FENAPEPRO by breaking their weak nationalist alignment with the players and seeking the assistance of their American senior partners, thus realigning Dominican baseball along class lines rather than national ones.

When free agency took hold in the United States the economic consequences were far-reaching and inadvertently contributed to the present crisis in Dominican baseball, for the astounding leap in players' salaries that free agency brought about contributed mightily to the refusal of Dominican major leaguers to play in their homeland. But Dominican baseball lacks the lucrative television contracts that the North American major leagues have and that underwrite the players' large salaries. Therefore if free agency comes to the Dominican Republic the likely beneficiaries will be the rank and file: those who play in the Dominican league and the American minor leagues and have spent little or no time in the major leagues. This could seriously disrupt the working relationship between major league teams and their Dominican counterparts, all of which depend on the ability of the owners of Dominican teams to

control their players. By strengthening the ranks of the journeymen
players, free agency might aid the Dominicans in their efforts to retain
control of their brand of baseball. On the other hand, it might further
weaken the structure of the Dominican professional league.

Whether free agency comes about will depend not on the number of
players who side with FENAPEPRO but rather on the caliber of players
who do. Until now few of the most successful Dominican players have
lent their support to FENAPEPRO; more will have to if the organization is
to succeed. Outside the Dominican Republic forces are at work that
might indirectly facilitate free agency. Expansion of the National
League, planned for 1992, will put pressure on the major league draft
system to enlarge its pool of prospects. Puerto Rico is part of the baseball
draft, and there are those who would like Dominican players to be included as well. To the degree that FENAPEPRO can cultivate good relations with other strata of Dominican baseball it could forge a stronger
position for itself and free agency. By working to systematize Dominican
baseball, making it more like North American baseball, FENAPEPRO can
emerge as the leader in the fight to modernize the game.

The struggle for free agency is taking place against a complex and
ever-changing background. On the surface the issue of free agency pits
players against owners, but in Dominican baseball class, culture, and
nationality are intricately interwoven: the Dominicans have tried to or-
ganize their game according to the guidelines laid down by the North
Americans but have succeeded only in part; the loyalties of the fans are
determined partly by their class but can also be swayed by press coverage; and the journalists are in turn professionals who might not be expected to aid the cause of resistance but who see themselves as subordi-
nates vis-à-vis the North Americans. It can be argued that nationalism
takes precedence over class on at least some ideological levels.

Just before the opening of the major league season in 1989, Epy
Guerrero caused a minor stir in the baseball world, and in Toronto in
particular, by publicly denouncing the Blue Jays for having treated Latino players unfairly. His charge that the Blue Jays denied Dominican
players the same opportunities for advancement, playing, and money
that they gave North Americans was surprising, in that Toronto has a
reputation for treating Dominicans better than any other team in baseball does: there are five Dominicans on the parent club and around forty
in the minor league system. Guerrero however maintained that some
sort of ceiling was now being imposed, that perhaps the Blue Jays had
become saturated with Latinos: "A serious problem has developed especially in the minor league system. I think its reached a point where the
organization can't handle so many Latin players. There's about forty

Latins in the organization. I think the managers, coaches, and trainers are tired of hearing so much Spanish." [74] More surprising still was that Guerrero went public so quickly. His aggressiveness shows not only that he understood how to use the news media but that he was unintimidated by so powerful a presence as the Blue Jays. When members of the Blue Jays' organization expressed surprise at his having gone to the press so quickly, he replied, "Sometimes you have to go to the press to bring the government down." [75]

Guerrero alleged that the organization had begun to brand Dominicans as "difficult," [76] and in an attempt to control them had alienated many of them: "Everyday now, it seems like there's some kind of problem with one of our Latin players. And I feel like I'm the bad guy because I'm the one who's been sending these players here . . . It's getting worse everyday. It started three years ago when Dámaso García was fighting with [Jimy] Williams [manager of the Blue Jays]. Then, last year there were problems between George Bell and Williams. In the minor leagues there were problems with Santiago García, and last year they sent Junior Felix home. Now, they're having a big problem with Jimy Kelly [Dominican shortstop] at the minor league complex here. They say he has a bad attitude and can't get along with managers." [77]

The incident involving Kelly prompted charges that the Blue Jays were anti-Dominican, as well as overt resistance on the part of the Dominicans. It was rumored that during spring training Kelly threw a baseball toward Toronto's vice president Bob Mattick, in apparent disgust at having been cut early from the Blue Jays' major league camp. The rumor so typified the mood at the time that whether it had any basis in fact is almost immaterial.

Guerrero's charges were backed by such successful Dominican players as Tony Fernández and George Bell. Bell's comments in the *Toronto Globe and Mail* showed that Dominicans as well as other Latinos were willing to confront the problem: "Latin players have been jumping all over me since I've been here because they feel they're not being treated fairly. And it's time for me to say something. Maybe the organization can start to realize the seriousness of the problem." [78]

Guerrero resorted to the same incendiary phrasing that American ballplayers use in their more acrimonious dealings with their clubs: "I'm gonna be a free agent [after this season]. Maybe I can find a club that appreciates me and my players." [79] That Guerrero sees himself both as a Dominican who has been wronged and as one who is able to stand up for himself is a sign of real resistance, his personal motives notwithstanding.

The self-destructive play of the Dominican team during post-season play in 1988–89 was reminiscent of the passive acts of sabotage by slaves in the antebellum South. After a stellar season the team was easily defeated in the championship series. There are many sports stories such as this: recall the Oakland A's in 1988 and the Los Angeles Lakers in 1989. But this time the relations between players and manager were unusually acrimonious, the manager was lacking in cultural sensitivity, and there were rumors in the press and occasional statements by the players to the effect that there was sabotage on the diamond. This made the story of the collapse of the Dominican team sadly atypical.

6

Quisqueya Qulture

An Ethnographic Sketch

● ● ● ● ● ● ● ●

Quisqueya Stadium opened in 1955, the same year Dominican baseball began its association with the major leagues, and a year that marked the onset of the modern era of Dominican baseball. Quisqueya has a special meaning for Dominicans: it is the country's premier baseball facility, its highest expression of the game. Since both teams in Santo Domingo (the Escogido Lions and the Licey Tigers) use the stadium and the rivalry between them is legendary, Quisqueya is the center of activity during most of the baseball season.

For parts of two seasons (1987–88 and 1988–89) I attended practice sessions and roughly forty games at Quisqueya Stadium, and met with baseball officials and other people in a variety of contexts. On the basis of my observations and interviews I compiled an ethnographic sketch of Quisqueya Stadium—a place that is both comparable to many North American stadiums and unlike any other.

Physical Setting

These days Quisqueya Stadium seems a bit run down. The poured concrete edifice is cracking, and paint is peeling away. People delicately complain about the hygiene, which is their polite way of saying the toilet facilities are bad. They feel that everything is in need of upgrading: from the loudspeaker system, which is so tinny that the Dominican national anthem is indistinguishable from the rum jingles that are played between innings, to the concession stands, which offer Dominican versions of Kentucky Fried Chicken (*Pica Pollo*). Quisqueya is really no worse than many a minor league stadium in the United States.

The dimensions of the stadium are respectable (nearly sixteen thousand seats) and so are those of the playing field, but in recognition of the relative scarcity of power hitters among Latin American players it is only four hundred feet to straightaway center field. The outfield walls are the first thing to make one realize that this is not an American ballpark, for next to advertisements for American products and companies (Coca-Cola, Texaco, Esso, Johnnie Walker) are interspersed others for Dominican ones (Barceló and Bermúdez rum, the Banco del Caribé, Presidente beer). But the difference between Quisqueya and other stadiums becomes clear only on the night of a game.

Only around the 1970s did scholarly attention begin to focus on the informal economy: the production and exchange of goods and services outside a society's normal and legitimate channels.[1] It is increasingly clear that in developing nations the establishment of a shadow economy is essential to most: "Governments tolerate or even stimulate informal economic activities as a way to resolve potential social conflicts or to promote political patronage. Such is the experience of most squatter settlements in Third World cities."[2] Studies of informal economies throughout Latin America have shown that to survive, family members pool their labor, some of which is extralegal.[3] That the informal economy flourishes at the stadium shows that the larger societal picture can often be grasped by observing its smaller units.

Scalpers and Tigeritos

Until the end of the season of 1987–88, as one turned off Tiradentes Avenue onto one of the smaller entrances to the park, one would pass a tiny shanty of maybe four little shacks thrown together beside a refuse heap about forty feet square. The children playing outside would be naked, and I remember one in particular. He always stood at the doorway with such a sad look in his eyes; a herniated navel protruded from his distended belly. The shacks stood in stark contrast to the stadium just behind, which dwarfed them. The shanty was a reminder to all who passed of the striking contrasts in the Dominican Republic: the displaced poor on one side of the huge wall of the stadium, the hope of fame and riches on the other. During night games the glow of the stadium lights made the dream of escape from poverty through baseball seem even more eerie, yet no less possible. When the Caribbean Series was held in Quisqueya Stadium at the end of the season of 1987–88, the government bulldozed the shanty so that it would not embarrass the country. But as I drive by I still cannot help seeing the outline of the little boy.

You get to the parking lot and are immediately met by someone unaffiliated with the stadium—no uniform, badge, or identification card—who will guide you to a parking spot, which is never hard to find, and watch your car for you. This is the "car watcher," a sort of human parking meter. The hand gesture for it all is an index finger moved to the eye, which is opened just slightly as if there were something in it to be cleared out. There is a tip expected for the service, as there is for everything in the country. The man may have a friend who will wash your car while you are at the game.

Before you have even got close to the gates, however, there are scalpers looking to sell you tickets to that night's game. Unlike scalpers in the United States, who operate clandestinely and illegally, Dominican scalpers work with the consent of the stadium management (though they are not formally retained by the management). They are given a number of tickets at various prices by the ticket office (they do not pay for them until later) and are allowed to sell them to anyone willing to pay. They try to get a higher price than is fetched at the ticket window and hope for tourists or for a well-attended game, when tickets are at a premium. Of course bargaining or haggling over the price is expected.

As you near the stadium a row of women are selling food: not the soft pretzels, hot dogs, and sausages that one finds at a North American ballpark, but oranges or grapefruits, peeled and ready to be eaten. Some people sell local candy, M&M's and Chicklets (the suggested dates of sale printed on the boxes have long expired), cheese, or small plastic whistles. There are always at least two vendors selling baseball caps bearing the emblems of the various Dominican teams. These hats are more poorly made than those found in the United States, but no one seems to care, and the price is right if you haggle. As you hand your ticket to the ticket taker and clear the turnstile you are greeted by members of the National Police, who in a nonbelligerent but insistent way search you and your bags. In North American major league parks there are security people who search bags at stadiums where there have been drinking problems, but they are usually dressed down and low-key so as not to rankle the fans. In Santo Domingo the police have M-16s, and they are not looking for alcohol (which you are permitted to bring in) but for weapons.

Having cleared the security force you are met by any of the scores of *tigeritos*, street urchins who show customers to their seats, which they wipe clean—for a fee, of course. (Like the scalpers the tigeritos work with the connivance of the stadium authorities.) Inside the stadium there are concession stands for pizza and fried chicken and beer, all locally produced.

The informal economy that is so clearly in evidence at the stadium stems from an understanding among the affluent that poverty is pervasive and that the rules ought to be relaxed. So, having paid for your car to be parked and perhaps washed, bought an overpriced ticket from a scalper and an orange from a vendor, and tipped a tigerito for being escorted to your seat, you have helped to support a variety of people who occupy the fringes of baseball and of the Dominican economy.

From Ice to Instant Replay: Vendors and Others

Unlike the car watchers, scalpers, and tigeritos, the vendors are employed by the stadium, as are the ticket sellers, ticket takers, and police. The people who make up the two branches of the stadium economy and social structure—the one formal and legal, the other informal and illegal—have much in common. They are of lower social and economic status, and many are illiterate and struggling to get by. Despite their different jobs, they all make roughly the same money. Most think nothing of inflating a price if they think they can get away with it, and even the police—especially the police—will pull you over on the pretext of some violation and expect a bribe. Rather than condemn or protest this behavior, most working-class Dominicans I asked justify bribes and price gouging because wages are so low.

By comparison, the rituals of the vendors in any North American major league park are as regular and synchronized as those of the guards at Buckingham Palace. The vendors hawk their merchandise to the crowd; yell back at them that you want a soft drink or a bag of peanuts, and they will pass you the drink or throw you the bag while you pass them the money. There is a sense of urgency in the transaction, as if you are taking money out of their pockets by taking too long—time is money. Even though Dominican vendors similarly get paid more if they sell more, they seem much more relaxed and less pressured, as Dominican life is in general. While selling as many drinks as possible is important, it does not take precedence over social interactions and love of the game.

By watching the vendors one can learn something of Dominican culture. Vendors are men and women, old and young. They do not wear any distinguishing hats or jackets but do have laminated cards with their photographs on them. They sell drinks (soft drinks, beer, and rum), candies, fried chicken, and pizza. Their attitude about their jobs and their behavior toward customers reveal several interesting cultural patterns and further distinguish them from their American counterparts.

When a customer orders a drink, typically the vendor will first use a bottle of soda or beer to smash a large chunk of ice, fragments of which shower the customers (this is a special treat on a hot night), then fill a plastic cup with the ice and the drink. The vendor will wait until the customer has drunk the whole bottle, so that the customer can return it to him. The vendor never seems hurried, will chat with the customers about almost anything, sometimes flirt with them; one woman showed me a picture of her youngest child and spoke with me for a full five minutes about him. Often after making a transaction a vendor will sit down near a customer and begin talking about the game.

Unlike North American stadiums, those in the Dominican Republic do not have large television screens, so vendors take on the function of instant replay. After an interesting or contested play they will often mime in the most animated way what has just occurred on the field, and the crowd will either shout its approval or argue. Once a shortstop made a remarkably strong throw from behind second base, and the runner was out by a quarter of a step. The stadium erupted, with some of the fans cheering and others feeling cheated: "The vendor in the aisle drops his bucket and screams with pride, 'What an arm! How strong! He is from the Cibao [central part of the country].' He imitates the throw and run. Others start arguing with him, 'He's dumb because he's from the Cibao. He's a countryman [bumpkin]. All he needs to do is wear his hat to the side.' Then, they all laugh uproariously."[4]

The relaxed pace of the game and of the people in the stands is complemented by trust in the area of economic exchanges. In all my time at the ballpark and all my transactions with vendors it was always implicit that I would pay my bill. Rather than have each fan pay for each transaction, a vendor will keep a tab going and pick it up in the later innings or as the fan leaves (provided of course that the fan looks trustworthy). What makes this remarkable is that the vendor may have several of these tabs going at once, in addition to having some customers pay for each item. Sometimes a tab will be begun because the vendor does not have any change; at other times it will be done as a courtesy. In either case, once the tab has been established the vendor will return every inning or two to see if the fan needs anything more. Only once did I see a customer try to walk out without paying. He was a big man and the vendor was a small, pregnant woman. She confronted him like a mongoose confronting a cobra, with the most vicious and expressive face I have ever seen. She went toe to toe with the man, and while pushing him with her low-slung belly not only demanded the money due but ridiculed him in front of the fans, who began to berate him. At first the man denied that he owed the vendor any money, but he ended up smiling sheepishly and paying her.

In addition to selling food and commenting on the game, the vendors are a source of entertainment. During the Championship Series of 1988–89 a merengue band was hired to play before the game and between innings. The musicians were stationed in the upper reaches of the stadium and provided with an excellent sound system. What happened was especially interesting to an outsider. During each inning the vendors went about their business and moved through the crowd, to the accompaniment of fans screaming and announcers announcing. When the final out of each half-inning was made the band struck up a fast merengue number, and after only a few notes the vendors (as well as other fans) stepped from the profane world of commerce to the sacred world of the merengue. The change happened so instantaneously and naturally that I was thrown by it. The vendors interrupted their work only for the millisecond that it took for them to begin moving to the music. Whether taking the money or cracking ice, they shook their heads and shuffled their feet to the familiar rhythm. They seemed like cheerleaders, starting and stopping the action while the fans joined in from their seats.

The scalpers and tigeritos have their counterparts in an illicit but accepted group of vendors. These are usually children from six to thirteen years of age, many of them homeless, who roam the stadium gathering empty bottles and selling *mani* (small packets of roasted peanuts that they prepare and package at home, or wherever they happen to be living). These children are essentially more enterprising tigeritos. Although scuffles between vendors, tigeritos, and others occasionally break out, for the most part Dominicans seem accepting of their attempts to make a go of it.

Bookies and Bobbies

When I attended my first game at Quisqueya I noted a group of about fifty people congregating in the upper reaches of the stadium. They made themselves conspicuous by standing throughout the game. A friend noticed that I was paying attention to them and chuckled. "That's Wall Street," he said. When I asked my friend what he meant he explained that a section of the stadium is given over to the placing of bets. Taking book is illegal, yet it goes on in full view of all those present, the authorities included. I made a point of spending one game in the bookies' area. What goes on there can only be described as a frenzy. Everything is bet on: the game, the next inning, the next pitch: "$50 on the second [pitch]!" Here is a knot of men, handing back and forth twenty-peso and hundred-peso notes, screaming at the top of their lungs about everything that happens on the field. I found out after asking repeated questions that the bookies lack the blessings of the authorities, even though they use the stadium as if they owned it. Once the bookies were cleaned out, arrested, and taken from the stadium in a paddy wagon. Within hours they were back, having used their very substantial political connections to win their freedom. Those who are supposed to watch out for illegality, such as the many police patrolling the vicinity, are routinely and publicly paid off.

The police seem omnipresent in the Dominican Republic, in large part because a job in the armed forces or in the national or local police is the only one many people can get. It is quite routine for there to be about a hundred police officers at Quisqueya; one told me that to be assigned to the stadium is choice duty (as I had suspected). In all my time at the stadium the police seemed to be needed only twice, when there were brawls. It is in fact hard to say whether the presence of the police works to discourage fights and criminality, or whether the Dominicans are nonviolent by their very nature. Dominicans are not bellicose but rather highly expressive (see below), and they rarely resort to violence with the ease that Americans do. (Of course this may soon change, since Dominicans are increasingly bringing back to their homeland the more violent values and life styles of New York.) But even if the presence of the police at Quisqueya does not help, it certainly cannot hurt.

The Fans

The Dominicans who now attend games tend to be a bit more well-off than those who did in the past. A ticket to a game has become a luxury; in a city where the electrical power can be interrupted for twelve hours a day, people are afraid to leave their homes for the evening; and transportation to and from the ballpark is erratic. Dominicans with cars or money for cabs can go and can afford the higher ticket prices. But the small middle-class in the Dominican Republic is increasingly hard-pressed to attend games as they once did, and the poor are relegated more than ever to hearing about them.

It seems odd at first to see a baseball stadium filled with blacks. Odd, that is, to someone from the United States, where black attendance at most major league parks is not very high.[5] There is also a different sense of fashion-consciousness at Quisqueya: less North American high fashion and more clothing in traditional Caribbean styles. It is striking that fashion, a cultural phenomenon easily transplanted and at times slavishly followed in the Dominican Republic, should be thwarted at the

ballpark:

> I see about me T-shirts with logos on them that are five years out
> of date, cheap imitations of Lacoste shirts, and other fairly tradi-
> tional styles of clothing, that would be shunned by many Domin-
> icans and, in the U.S., by African-Americans who are more
> stylish. There is also an effort by women to color their hair in an
> attempt to imitate American popular culture heroes. The impos-
> sibility of all but the rich to buy the latest American fashions
> dooms their attempts at high fashion to cheap imitations that are
> bound to be off. Sometimes they're off a little as with that woman
> two rows in front of me who is wearing black boots attempting to
> look like her fashion counterpart in the U.S. (Western cowboy
> look—metal strip around the toe and decorative stitching). How-
> ever, hers have additional chains and rhinestone baubles on them
> and exaggerate the style she's looking to emulate. Others really
> miss. It's when Americans (Black or White) walk by that I see the
> differences most—the ability to buy a better grade of clothing and
> more refined styles is immediately apparent.[6]

Typical articles of Dominican dress for men include the *guayabera* (a
dress shirt worn loosely outside the pants), a variation on dress pants,
and shoes that resemble loafers. Women emulate North American fashions more than men do, but they seem to dress more conservatively
than women in the United States. A Dominican or American woman
wearing jeans at the stadium causes heads to turn.

If Americans in the Dominican Republic dress more expensively and
more casually than the natives (they are often readily distinguishable because of their affinity for wearing shorts), they still cannot match the
ease with which Dominicans—and most non-Westerners—carry themselves. Body language can obliterate all the pretense of expensive clothing and the glitter of accoutrements. By being physically at ease, Dominicans of both sexes seem ever so much more elegant than their richer
neighbors from the northern hemisphere.

Another noteworthy feature of Quisqueya culture is the bipartisan
nature of the crowds. At almost any game there will be large blocks of
fans, sometimes half of those in attendance, who root for the visiting
team. This is most pronounced when the two teams from the capital
play against each other. There is nothing comparable in the United
States, for even the metropolitan areas that have two major league
teams have one in each league. North American fans are also more affluent, as is evident in the way they display allegiance to a team by wear-

ing its authentic, licensed paraphernalia: hats, jackets, baseball shirts. By comparison, in the Dominican Republic it is sufficient for fans to wear their team's color: if the team's color is blue the fans will wear anything blue—a blue ribbon from the family sewing basket or a blue checked shirt.

> January 25, 1989. Quisqueya Stadium. Crowd is big tonight. Merengue band going full tilt. I'm sitting almost right on the dividing line. To my left is blue [Licey], to my right red [Escogido]. Each side has its colors: homemade banners, hats, shirts, official and unofficial. Anything with the color is appropriate: Boston Red Sox hats, Detroit Tigers hats, New York Mets hats, all are worn by Licey fans [all forms of blue]. Escogido will wear St. Louis Cardinals' hats and Cincinnati Reds' hats. Hearing the game is like playing with the balance knob on your stereo. You'll hear it out of one ear or the other depending on who's doing what. Each time Licey goes down the Escogido fans to my right rise up en masse and, in a single voice, raise the roof at the same time the band clicks in and the dancing ensues. The entire right side of this place is swallowed up in joy.[7]

Dominican baseball is materially shabby, but it has a verve, an energy, and a pride that one does not see in the North American game. Many observers have noted this dynamic quality, which stems from culture rather than material wherewithal.[8]

Considerate Fanatics

The dynamism of Dominican baseball is part of a much larger cultural pattern of expressiveness. Dominican culture is considered even by other Latin Americans as relatively emotional, free, noisy, and spontaneous. This holds true for both men and women, at least among the lower and middle classes, which account for the great majority of the country. I noticed this expressiveness almost everywhere I went: at the stadium, in the academies, in the shopping plazas, and in the locker rooms and on the field, where the players would play the flip game[9] and let barbs and banter fly, all at a volume intended for everyone to hear. It is manifested in conversation (loud laughter, repartee, exclamations and explanations that take at least two full breaths) and in a penchant for banter and argument, profusely illustrated by hand gestures. It is most noticeable in the way people react to events. One former major leaguer described the cultural differences between Dominican and American players as follows: "You know how it is with us. We are loud. We would

stay up till late and play cards, and holler, and keep the other players
awake. That's why they room us together."[10]

In North American ballparks the fans are also given to expressions of
joy and anger, yells and chants, and the "wave." But Dominican fans
carry these forms of expression a notch or two further; it is this behavior,
unmediated by selfconsciousness, that characterizes Dominicans (and
most likely other Caribbean peoples). Where an ecstatic American fan
will give a "high five" to his friend or thrust his clenched fist into the air,
the Dominican *fanático* will routinely grab a stranger and chatter ef-
fusively about what has just happened. During one game that I attended
Escogido fans were interspersed among Licey fans in the middle sec-
tions of the stadium. After one particularly bad play by an Escogido
player, the Licey fans were joyous and demonstrative, blasting away on
their sirens and bullhorns. The Licey fan next to me reached over to an
Escogido fan one row up (the closest one he could find) and turned his
hat sideways, a mocking gesture meant to suggest stupidity or back-
wardness. The Escogido fan began some lively banter that was picked
up by other fans who did not know each other but happened to be sitting
nearby. Within seconds the Licey fans were recreating the play for the
Escogido fan and jumping up and down excitedly. They laughed so
hard that they were falling in each other's arms. The easy physicality of
these fans, most of whom were strangers, is quite different from the more
restrained camaraderie of American fans.

The male Dominican fan will also indulge in a range of behavior
broader than that considered acceptable for most North American males.
Machismo notwithstanding, he will jump up and down like a boy if he
is moved, and cry more easily—which I noticed at the stadium on a
number of occasions. Another sign of the culture of expressiveness is
that Dominican males are in some respects far less homophobic than
American males: while they frown on homosexuality because of their
highly developed sense of machismo, Dominican men can nevertheless
express closeness to other men; they feel no awkwardness about being
physically close to each other or touching each other. For instance, at
ballgames men who are sharing a secret will whisper to each other and
end up closer than North American standards of behavior would allow.
And at the academies the prospects greet each other with hugs and cry
when they say goodbye.

In a culture that stresses spontaneity and expressiveness people lead a
more fulfilling emotional and social life, but feelings are quickly and
easily hurt and tempers can get out of control. Although it is socially
loose and friendly, Caribbean culture and in particular Dominican cul-

ture have their explosive side. I noticed a telling example when I sat between the two camps of fans at one of the championship games between Escogido and Licey. Licey jumped into the lead, 2 to 0, and its fans were jubilant. Each time a Licey player made a hit or scored a run, the fans filled the stadium with cheers and Licey's colors. Those faithful to Escogido who were seated near them were subject to all manner of symbolic abuse, as the Licey fans made them relive their humiliations. The Escogido fan I happened to be in front of was a middle-aged man who was seated alone. His respectable appearance, dress, and demeanor obviously showed him to be a professional of some sort.[11] He smiled occasionally as he took the jibes of the Liceyistas, two of whom in particular were taunting him incessantly. Around the seventh inning Escogido got back on track and tied the game. When the team scored its first run the mild-mannered gentleman became an animal, snarling insults at the Licey fans at the top of his lungs. He lost all control as he drew closer to them and they to him. Having witnessed and been a party to several fracases in my years of attending sporting events, I was certain that the outburst would lead to blows. But it was as if some invisible barrier separated the two sides: they stood jawing away at each other but remained a foot apart. Other fans sat by and laughed as the baseball game and the insult game continued.

Clearly there was considerable verbal leeway between the combatants, and the verbal abuse and posturing that were a large part of the confrontation were intended to defuse emotions and energy. I had seen the same thing happen in several situations unrelated to baseball. I saw several other instances of this emotional bellicosity at Quisqueya, but only twice did it result in fights. This is remarkable considering that the Dominicans consume an enormous amount of alcohol at the games. Rum can be bought cheaply at the stadium—a sales representative for Barceló told me that his company could expect to sell four thousand bottles to a crowd of ten thousand—but most fans prefer to bring their own rum in hip flasks. The fans also drink potent beer at the stadium, and all this is in addition to what they have already drunk at home before the game.

That Dominicans are culturally predisposed to avoid chaos and violence was made even more clear one evening in December 1987. Santo Domingo had been experiencing electrical blackouts (*apagos*) since my arrival in early 1987. Usually the sites of such major spectacles as carnivals and baseball games had been spared, but one night when I was at Quisqueya the lights went dark in the middle of a game with the score tied and the stadium filled with inebriated fans. At the time I was standing at the entrance to a ramp. The blackout happened so quickly and

was so complete that the effect was like that of entering a theater during
a movie: it takes a minute or so for the eyes to adjust to the darkness, and
in a crowded stadium that minute can be frightening. Oddly, there were
no screams or throngs making for the exits. Instead thousands of people
lit their lighters and matches. Someone had his radio tuned to a merengue station, and people just lingered, some dancing, most continuing to
drink and laugh. Once I realized that nothing horrible would happen in
the dark, mobbed stadium, I imagined how the same occurrence in my
home town of Boston or elsewhere might have had less fortunate consequences. I shuddered to think of what thirty thousand Red Sox fans
would do at Fenway Park, or forty thousand Met fans at Shea Stadium.

The cultural differences between Dominicans and North Americans
were brought home to me when I attended the Caribbean Series in
Miami in 1990. More than a thousand fans came from the Dominican
Republic, and along with their compatriots already in Florida they
made a jubilant and raucous crowd. The Miami Police Department,
charged with overseeing the event, showed their misunderstanding of
cultural differences by wading into the crowd of revelers and arresting
people. The Dominicans were shocked and outraged at what they took
to be cruel and arbitrary harassment. They tried to protest, but the police felt threatened by their excitability and raised voices. At home no
one would have batted an eye at the merrymakers; in Miami they were
seen as a menace.

Dominican culture differs markedly from Euro-American culture in
one other important respect: its elastic conception of punctuality. Dominicans will typically arrive twenty minutes late for a meeting; they
will also arrive late for a movie, and will immediately begin talking to
the screen in response to lines delivered by the actors, even if they have
no notion of the plot; and they will arrive late for a ballgame, sometime
between the start and the third inning.

I have come to think of Dominicans as an interesting combination of
passion and consideration. Despite their excitability, in some ways Dominican fans seem more even-tempered than North American fans,
and by extension than North American society. The juxtaposition of
passion, alcohol, and a hotly contested game should make anyone wary
of attending a Dominican ballgame. But Dominican culture fashions a
terrain on which verbal and body language are the weapons of confrontation: the ego is bloodied, but the opponent is left physically intact.
Dominicans have ample opportunity to come to blows, but they do not.
I would have to conclude that they are more social than North Americans, more in tune with human frailty. Because they see so much human vulnerability, because they are closer to the margins of life, they

are more likely to resist the urge to bully and harm. These are merely observations, not tested hypotheses; but sometimes a single insight is worth more than a thousand correlations. In any event, one can learn a lot about culture from watching a baseball game.

The Players

In one sense the players are culturally the least isolated group in baseball, for they have had more exposure to North American life than the fans, tigeritos, vendors, bookies, or scalpers. On the other hand, Dominican ballplayers at home are more free to be themselves, to be Dominican, than when they play in the United States. This was poignantly brought home to me one night as I interviewed Dominican players on the field before a game. In two interviews players who spoke English feigned ignorance of it and made me interview them in Spanish. Perhaps they were joking or deliberately being rude, but more likely they felt that gringos should use the language of those being interviewed, especially on the home turf of those being interviewed. This conviction bespeaks a consciousness of being at home, and the willingness to act on it is a form of cultural resistance.

The most striking thing about the players is how loose they seem. There is none of the regimentation, guardedness, and nervous tension that characterizes players in the United States. North American managers must take this looseness into account when they go to the Caribbean, for the players' conception of the game and of time is as elastic as that of other Dominicans: if batting practice is called for five o'clock the players may not show up until ten or twenty minutes later, and the bigger names may not show up at all.[12]

The loose character of Winter League baseball is also evident in the joking and little games of the athletes. The flip game is almost always being played. Every evening I saw clusters of three to five players swatting the ball among themselves with their gloves until one missed the ball and it fell to the ground. The players shrieked with laughter and expletives and challenged each other one on one, at times betting on the outcome. Thinking this was public behavior for the benefit of the fans, I was mildly surprised when I went into the clubhouse and saw the flip game being played in the crowded locker room. Those not playing were sitting around drinking shot glasses of strong Dominican coffee and yelling as loudly as those who were tapping the ball around.

One reason the Dominicans play so intensely and yet are so much at ease is that they are playing at home, in their element. It is the North Americans who are the visitors:

I still feel special when I'm at Quisqueya. I went here when I was a little boy, and now, some of the same people I was in the stands with, come to see me. I can't believe it sometimes.[13]

Back in the States, we're just Latinos. Here I'm always playing in front of my country[men]. They cheer for us like no one [else].[14]

During the championship series, when the merengue band was playing before the game and between at-bats, a number of the ballplayers were dancing while batting or throwing. They were joined by several fans who leaped on top of the dugout and on the field to the peculiar merengue shuffle. The Americans stood by stiffly, and suddenly it became clear how Dominican the game really was.

The casualness of Dominican baseball extends to security, which before a game is almost nonexistent. Journalists roam about in search of interviews, children loiter, and fans without press credentials seem to have access to the field and the players.

Baseball at Quisqueya has many peculiarly local traditions. One custom is a Dominican variation of the North American "seventh-inning stretch": a young man named Torito runs out on the field, carrying on his back a stuffed tiger three feet tall (to symbolize the Licey Tigers), and circles the bases at a dead run, sliding into home. There are also less institutionalized forms of unusual behavior on the field. The players do not seem to mind when an exuberant child or two runs onto the field, or when a *bruja* (witch) is used by one team against the other, or when a transvestite and a partner do the merengue on top of the dugout or along the first-base line. None of the interruptions are long, and all the people seem to want to keep the flow of the game going as well as to make their statement. Dominicans have a sense of the extravagant gesture that makes their style of baseball dramatic. They also know that the press and their friends will be critical if they appear sluggardly. This is enough inducement for many to indulge in their unique theatrics, while the Americans can get by (not that they all do) with less emotionality, more circumscribed gestures, stiffness, selfconsciousness.

At Quisqueya one sees a North American game that has been Dominicanized. The game remains American in structure, but its setting is Dominican and it has become infused with Dominican values. Victor Turner has pointed out that performance not only reflects culture but is a form of critique.[15] Quisqueya is more than a sporting venue: it is also the site of a mass spectacle that makes simultaneous use of American and Dominican elements. Admittedly these American elements are often included because those who represent American interests are watching, and in any event the American elements are often Dominicanized. But it is essential nonetheless that the elements be present if the performance is to have the effect of a critique of North American culture. This critical function is reciprocal: baseball at Quisqueya embodies many of the things that North Americans find blameworthy in Dominican culture—lateness, overly casual behavior, inefficiency. But the Dominicans see these characteristics as a source of pride, and they take their game seriously.

During batting practice one day at Quisqueya Stadium I watched the vendors prepare for another day of work. I signaled to one and ordered a soft drink. After the vendor had given me my drink and taken my money, she smiled and to my surprise made the sign of the cross. Not twenty minutes later I bought something from another vendor, one whom I knew, and she too made the sign of the cross. I asked a friend who was with me what the reason for this was, and after jokingly suggesting that I looked like Jesus Christ he explained that it was believed to be good luck to have a gringo as a first customer. The same vendor eagerly goes after North Americans since they are so easily shortchanged. Hence while North Americans are reviled they are also venerated; the Dominican attitude toward them is one of simultaneous approach and avoidance.

The Dominicans view progress as being tied to American styles of life and culture, yet they cannot help but infuse whatever they do with some of their own culture, even at the expense of ruining their efforts at assimilation. In the stadium, for example, there are attempts at making the game appear as slick as the North American version, but Dominicanisms keep cropping up. One middle-aged vendor whom I spoke to liked to think that he was selling trendy items to the fans. All evening he wound his way up and down the aisle, carrying baskets filled with little whistles that never worked. When I asked him why he was selling these worthless items rather than team pennants, he told me that his nephew had many whistles in San Pedro. I told the man that he could make more money with pennants, but he only nodded and said, "But it's my nephew."

7

Sugarball

A Bittersweet

Game

● ● ● ● ●

The game of baseball is a filter through which various influences pass. Culture, society, and politics color the sport, calling into question the view that baseball is simply the "American" pastime, the sport that reflects America's mainstream values.

Caribbean baseball is rooted in colonialism. The game began as a seasonal diversion for sugar cane cutters urged on them by their employers.[1] Its popularity grew as North American political, military, and economic domination of the Dominican Republic increased. Later the managers of refineries in the sugar cane regions of the east offered cash payments to cane cutters so as to field good teams, which soon competed on a high level. The workers chose to take part as much because of the material rewards as because of the time they could spend away from the cane fields. In the cities baseball had been introduced earlier, by Cuban immigrants, and was quickly picked up by local schools and companies, who made it into a semiprofessional sport.

In the early 1950s the high caliber of Dominican play finally came to the attention of North American major league teams, who saw the Dominican Republic as a talent bonanza and moved quickly to usurp control of the game. The major league clubs did not see this as expropriation: they never saw Latin American baseball as anything but a backwater, and believed they were doing the poor people there a favor by giving them an opportunity to play ball in the major leagues—an opportunity for which most North Americans would have given anything, and one that the Dominicans welcomed just as eagerly.

In the thirty-five years since the North Americans began to work closely with Dominican professional baseball teams, the major league talent that the Dominican Republic has provided has surpassed all expectations. The working relationships that Dominican professional teams established with American major league clubs secured and helped develop local prospects. Both nations have benefited from the collaboration: the United States for the contributions to its major league game in the summer, the Dominican Republic for the contributions to its own league in the winter. But the academies established by the North Americans undercut the traditional role of Dominican amateur baseball as a developer of talent, and the advent of free agency in the United States had the unforeseen effect of discouraging Dominican stars from taking part in winter play. American baseball was unwittingly curbing the precarious autonomy of Dominican baseball and weakening its structure from both the top and the bottom. The result was a direct dependence on major league teams, much like the dependence on American corporations that characterizes other sectors of Dominican society. The political and economic domination of the game had an ideological consequence: the passing on of the belief that culture in general and baseball in particular was better in the United States than in the Dominican Republic.

The Resistance of Dominican Baseball

Dominican resistance has taken many forms: the military expulsion of the Haitians in the nineteenth century, successful guerrilla war against the United States in the early twentieth century, and the development of a national culture. Taking on the sport of baseball aided national cultural movements. Dominicans infused the game with their own raucous, melodramatic style, marked by a highly individualistic way of playing, an easygoing attitude toward the game both on the field and in the stands, music and dancing, and crowds by turns temperamental and tranquil.

The Dominican attitudes toward Americans, the curious mix of approach and avoidance, reflect the tension between hegemony and resistance. Dominicans want to reduce the sociocultural and economic distance that separates them from the North Americans, but they also want to thwart the presence of the United States. They want to express national pride yet ape the North Americans. The news media play a special role. Baseball journalists have become the gatekeepers of Dominican nationalism, for they carefully direct criticism away from criollos—native players—and toward the North Americans who control them. Although the fans recognize the superiority of American major league play, they still prefer their own brand of béisbol on nationalistic

grounds. When the game is played at home the players show their cultural pride by demanding to play the game at their own tempo and in their own style, and they will engage in passive resistance if their demands are not met. Ironically, the most overt resistance comes from those players who are most successful and have the most to lose.

Resistance through Sport

My study of how Dominicans adapted the sport of baseball fits into a small but growing field of literature on resistance through sport. Others have also argued that sport is an appropriate terrain for cultural resistance. In the mid-1970s the sports sociologists Richard Gruneau, John Hargreaves, and Ian Taylor, along with others at the Center for Contemporary Cultural Studies in Birmingham, England, began to formulate the issue of sport as hegemony and later of sport as resistance.[2] In their view the history of British soccer—and more recently of soccer hooliganism—is the history of efforts by the English working class to dramatize their grievances, assert their cultural autonomy, and state their opposition to dominant British society: "Without some notion of the autonomy of popular cultural tradition and of the power of subordinate groups to resist manipulation and control from above, manifestations of conflict and resistance involving people who are also sports enthusiasts cannot be explained. The development of football in Britain illustrates this point."[3]

Most studies of sport as cultural resistance have been made by social historians. Within this burgeoning field are studies of sport as the focus of conflict between classes,[4] and other studies (like mine) of sport as a symbol of foreign domination.[5]

The use of foreign symbols as tools against foreigners and the growth of national pride are inextricable. In his study of Meiji Japan, Donald Rhoden looked at the ironic function of baseball in the country's quest for national identity.[6] The bringing of the game to Asia was to be the cultural concomitant of the expansion of the United States: "to follow the flag" was the way baseball's first promoter and entrepreneur, A. J. Spaulding, put it. While Americans played the game with each other and encouraged the Japanese to play it among themselves, American feelings of racial and cultural superiority prevented them from playing against the Japanese. After repeated invitations, the Americans at the Yokohama Athletic Club in May 1896 played against the boys of Ichiko (a university preparatory academy in Japan). The string of rejections that the Japanese had received to their invitations only increased their resentment, and the game "assumed the dimensions of a righteous struggle for national honor."[7] To everyone's surprise the Americans lost badly, and lost a rematch and then a third game. With each victory the boys of Ichiko were heralded as giant killers who excelled at the Americans' national game, all of which fed the need for national identity in a changing Japan.

Joseph's study of the Yucatecan working class shows how baseball promoted socialist class identity during the Mexican Revolution.[8] As in England and elsewhere, sport was initially the province of the wealthy. In the Yucatán in 1890 it was the urban elite who first took on the game, in imitation of foreign fashion.[9] The working class did not gain any real access to baseball until just after the turn of the century, when with the rise of the henequen market the oligarchy sought to entertain and appease its workers by promoting the sport among them.[10] The workers took the game for their own; later the socialist candidates wanted to further their own political goals by promoting the sport as an instrument of class solidarity. Baseball can clearly be used for direct political ends in addition to being used indirectly to foment class conflict and promote cultural control. David LaFrance has noted the enormous pride Mexicans felt during Fernando Valenzuela's first seasons with the Los Angeles Dodgers.[11] The Mexican press appears to have played the same role as the Dominican press does in inspiring nationalism. LaFrance argues that the press used the success of Mexican players in baseball to bludgeon the Americans, whom they tended to fault for perceived wrongs committed against Valenzuela. This style of reporting kept the readership in a state of perpetual turmoil during the "Fernandomania" of 1982–84.[12]

Studies of sport in the Caribbean have been much less common. Trinidad and Tobago, where baseball is not played, was the site of a study by Mandle and Mandle of how basketball was altered to frame local cultural issues.[13] No discussion of sport in the Caribbean is complete without the mention of C. L. R. James;[14] his pioneering work on Jamaican cricket is a classic study of resistance, reflecting much of the ideological and psychological ambivalence that is relevant to resistance.

Baseball and Symbolic Analysis

In some ways Dominican data suggest the concept of "bricolage" used by Lévi-Strauss,[15] Hebdige,[16] and Clark.[17] Bricolage is the placing of objects in a new context, to convey new meaning within a conventional system. For example, a punk rocker will make a common safety pin into a symbol of resistance by wearing it in his cheek. It is as much the commonness of the object as the new context that makes it significant. In the Dominican Republic the primary object is the sport of baseball and the secondary objects are the symbols associated with it. North American institutions, ideology, and symbols dominate most areas of Dominican life and Dominicans are made to feel culturally inferior, but the symbols associated with baseball can be taken from the North Americans and become the pride of the Dominicans. A milk carton can be flattened and fashioned into a mitt, a tree branch or sugar cane stalk into a bat. These become powerful symbols of success against seemingly insurmountable odds. North Americans coming to the Dominican Republic are invariably touched by the youngsters and their milk cartons. While preferring a real mitt or a nice wooden bat, Dominican boys know that even with their makeshift implements they will one day perform wonders. In baseball Dominican boys have a dignity. Not only does their poverty fail to detract from their accomplishments and dreams, but it adds to their sense of pride. Thousands of young Dominicans are inspired by stories like that of Tony Fernández, who once regularly scampered over the outfield wall of the stadium in San Pedro de Macorís to shag flies and now plays for the Toronto Blue Jays.

A baseball game is in many respects akin to a performance of another kind, like a play, a concert, or a film. What happens on the playing field is only one part of the performance: the fans, the noise, and the music are also part of it, and they are what make the game uniquely Dominican.

One reason why baseball at Quisqueya Stadium is such a spectacle is that the game is being played in front of foreigners, and everyone is aware of this. Scouts, coaches, managers, and owners from North American teams regularly attend games to look over their prospects and those of the competition. North American and Japanese journalists regularly cover Dominican baseball. Rather than conceal their culture or modify it to accommodate the foreigners, the Dominicans parade their cultural excesses in front of them.

Fanning the Flames

The Dominican press has seized on the inequalities between major league teams and their Dominican affiliates and played up the interference of the major league teams in Dominican baseball. It has criticized especially strongly the pressure that North Americans exert on Dominican players to leave crucial series before they are over when the players are needed elsewhere; the North American managers seem insensitive to the Dominican dimension of the game. The press refuses to overlook these slights. In addition to making much fanfare of Dominican accomplishments in the major leagues it derides North Americans for their cultural insensitivity. This combines with the many Dominican elements of the game and its fans to usurp baseball for Dominican ends. The flames of nationalist resentment are not difficult to fan considering the history of American intervention in the country.

As Brecht[18] and Benjamin[19] both argued, mass culture can promote repressive movements or revolutionary ones, but which road it will take is never a foregone conclusion. Sport in Latin America has a greater capacity for radical political or cultural expression than it does in the United States, where it is generally seen as a benign reflex of a conservative system and as a reflection of a conservative world view.

Having struggled in obscurity to refine the game Dominicans have made it their own, a game marked by their cadence and color. Dominicans poured their love into their own players, gladiators who triumphed in the United States. Each title won by a Dominican in the major leagues is a coup for his compatriots at home struggling to get by. The Dominicans have pushed many things into the background as they wait for their heroes to triumph against the Americans. They stumble through the darkened streets of Santo Domingo and put up with runaway prices, but in baseball they are more assertive. The Dominicans are a beleaguered people who may someday rebel; to predict when the flash point will occur, look first to the firefights being waged in a game that has inspired their confidence. Look first at sugarball.

Appendix

Ethnographic Methods

● ● ● ● ● ● ● ●

Carrying out research in as large a geographic area as I studied for this book requires an array of methods that go beyond traditional ethnography, and a comment on the methods I used is in order.

At the baseball academy Campo Las Palmas it was possible for me to rely almost exclusively on ethnographic field methods because of the closed nature of the site: everyone lived and functioned in a confined space and a bounded social universe. Almost all the interviews with the players were conducted in Spanish, those with the staff in English. I made observations about all phases of life at the academy. I was there for workouts, games, tryouts, classes, and leisure hours. I followed some players as they left the camp during the week and on weekends. I helped conduct their English classes, even providing them with an instructor and at times acting in that capacity myself. I conducted both formal and field interviews at the academy.

Other phases of my research demanded many different methods. To clarify the relations of different levels of the game (amateur baseball, professional baseball), at times I needed to outline the structure of the game. To do this I needed to conduct formal interviews. At other times when I was at Quisqueya Stadium I would use a combination of informal interviews (referred to as field interviews in the notes below) and formal ones, supplemented by my observations. On occasion I used survey questionnaires as well, especially when I needed to generalize about populations in widely separate areas. At other times I worked with textual materials, as when I did a content analysis of Dominican newspapers or looked into popular positions on baseball issues.

QUESTIONNAIRE USED IN SAN PEDRO DE MACORIS
28 March 1987   Sample: 100 males
 1. Name
 2. Age [ranged from 16 to 32]

3. Occupation [30 unemployed, 53 unskilled laborers, 16 semiskilled laborers, 1 baseball scout]

4. Education [6 graduated high school, 10 had some high school, 84 had no high school]

5. Baseball playing experience [6 played informally, 94 played in formal leagues]

6. Future expectations (what will you be doing in ten years?)

7. Does he have a friend (rather than an acquaintance) who has signed with an American team? [86 have friends who signed]

8. Does he have a relative who has signed with an American team? [12 have relatives who signed; only 2 have neither friends nor relatives who signed]

9. If you were paid 100 pesos a day would you agree to cut cane for 5 years? [59 no, 41 yes]

10. If you were paid 300 pesos a day would you agree to cut cane for 5 years? [35 no, 65 yes]

QUESTIONNAIRE USED AT QUISQUEYA STADIUM AND
IN TWO NEIGHBORHOODS IN SANTO DOMINGO
8–10 January 1988   Sample: 164 respondents

1. Which is your favorite major league team in the United States?
2. Which is your favorite team here in the Dominican Republic?
3. If you had to choose a hat to wear from only one of these teams [price and quality were the same], which would you pick?
4. Why did you pick this hat?
5. What is your age?
6. What do you do for a living?
7. What town or neighborhood do you live in?

SAMPLE DIALOGUES FROM THE ROOKIES' CLASS
IN ENGLISH AS A SECOND LANGUAGE,
CAMPO LAS PALMAS, 1988

The Restaurant

Waitress: "Hi boys! What'll it be?" or "Would you like to see a menu?"

Players: "I'd *like* a cheeseburger and fries."

"I will have a salad and soup, please."

[It is important to remember that in the United States you ask for things more politely than in the Dominican Republic. *DON'T* order: "Give me a cheeseburger."]

Waitress: "Are you gonna have anything to drink?"

Players:	"Yes, *I'll have* a coke."
	"*I'd like* coffee with cream."
[Later:]	
Waitress:	"Will there be anything else?" or "Do *you want* more coffee?"
Players:	"No, thank you."
	"We would *like* the check."

Leave a tip . . .

Key verbs: querer = want

desear = desire (meaning to like, to want but softer)

tener = to have

The Police

You are walking down the street in a town or rural city in the U.S. The police don't see people who are not white very often. They may think you are suspicious, or just may want to find out what you are doing.

Police:	"Hello boys. New in town?"
Players:	"Yes. *We are* ballplayers."
Police:	"Can I *see* some identification?"
Players:	"Sure (take out identification), here you are."
Police [satisfied]:	"Thanks. Who you playin' for?"
Players:	"*We play* for the Los Angeles Dodgers."
Police:	"Where are ya headin' for now?"
Players:	"We are *looking* for a (movie, restaurant)."
	"We are *going* for a walk."

Key verbs: ser = to be

mirar = to look

ir = to go

jugar = to play

This is accompanied by a brief talk on how race is perceived in the United States. Lighter-skinned Dominicans have a hard time understanding that they are perceived as black when they get there.

Notes

INTRODUCTION

1 Glen Macnow, "The Boys of Winter," *Detroit Free Press*, 4 February 1986, p. 3.
2 Alan M. Klein, "Pumping Irony: Crisis and Contradiction in Bodybuilding Subculture," *Sport Sociology Journal* 3 (1986): 112–34.
3 Jay Coakley, *Sport in Society: Issues and Controversies*, 4th ed. (Times Mirror/Mosby, 1990).
4 The first major work on stacking was Arnold Rosenblatt, "Negroes in Baseball: The Failure of Success," *Transaction* 4 (1967): 51–63.

CHAPTER ONE
Overview and Origins

1 Thomas E. Weil et al., *The Dominican Republic: A Country Study* (Washington: U.S. Government Printing Office, 1982), 16; Howard J. Wiarda and Michael Kryzanek, *The Dominican Republic: A Caribbean Crucible* (Boulder: Westview, 1982), 9.
2 Ibid., 19.
3 Ibid., 16.
4 Jan Knepper Black, *The Dominican Republic: Politics and Development in an Unsovereign State* (Boston: Allen and Unwin, 1986), 58.
5 Wiarda and Kryzanek, *Dominican Republic*, 96.
6 Santo Domingo lost its *audiencia*, or position as the seat of the Royal Court of Appeals, which was moved to more prosperous colonies on the mainland. Black, *Dominican Republic*, 14.
7 Roger Plant, *Sugar and Modern Slavery: A Tale of Two Countries* (London: Zed Books, 1987), 5.
8 Ibid., 5.
9 Ibid., 6.
10 Ibid., 6.
11 Ibid., 7.
12 The *encomienda* was a land grant entitling its recipient to use the land (though not own it), along with the labor of the natives on it.
13 Cuban, Puerto Rican, and Dominican politics have affected each other profoundly. Historically, disenfranchised groups and individuals have fled

from one island to another, and brought their native ways of life to their new homes.

14 José del Castillo, "The Formation of the Dominican Sugar Industry: From Competition to Monopoly, from National Semiproletariat to Foreign Proletariat," in *Between Slavery and Free Labor: The Spanish Speaking Caribbean in the Nineteenth Century*, ed. Manuel Fraginals et al. (Baltimore: Johns Hopkins University Press, 1985), 215.

15 Ibid., 217.

16 Plant, *Sugar and Modern Slavery*, 15.

17 Bruce Calder, *The Impact of Intervention: The Dominican Republic during the U.S. Occupation of 1916–1924* (Austin: University of Texas Press, 1984), 3.

18 Ibid., xii.

19 Wiarda and Kryzanek, *Dominican Republic*, 34.

20 Plant, *Sugar and Modern Slavery*, 20.

21 Wiarda and Kryzanek, *Dominican Republic*, 36.

22 Black, *Dominican Republic*, 28.

23 Wiarda and Kryzanek, *Dominican Republic*, 43.

24 Catherine Sunshine, *The Caribbean: Survival, Struggle, and Sovereignty* (Boston: South End Press, 1988), 150.

25 Ibid., 151.

26 Ibid., 153.

27 Mark Kurlansky, "The Dominican Republic's Two Caudillos," *San Francisco Chronicle*, 9 August 1989.

28 Weil et al., *Dominican Republic*, 40.

29 Castillo, "Formation of Dominican Sugar," 215.

30 Plant, *Sugar and Modern Slavery*, 13.

31 Ibid., 15.

32 Donald Rhoden, "Baseball and the Quest for National Identity in Meiji Japan," *American Historical Review* 85 (1980): 511–34.

33 Fernando Vicioso and M. Alvarez, *Béisbol dominicano, 1891–1967* (Santo Domingo, 1967), 12.

34 Interview, Santo Domingo, 29 January 1989.

35 Vicioso and Alvarez, *Béisbol dominicano*, 13.

36 Ibid., 13.

37 Ibid., 13.

38 Ibid., 15.

39 Cúqui Córdova, *Album del recuerdo*, 1 (Santo Domingo, 1983): 85.

40 Vicioso and Alvarez, *Béisbol dominicano*, 14.

41 Ibid., 14.

42 Interview, Campo Las Palmas, 20 December 1987.

43 Interview, Santo Domingo, 29 January 1989.

44 Vicioso and Alvarez, *Béisbol dominicano*, 14.

45 Cúqui Córdova, "Nestor Lambertus fué 'chivo expiatorio' en el campeonato de 1922," *Listin diario* (Santo Domingo), 13 June 1987.

46 Ibid.

47 Córdova, *Album del recuerdo*, 4 (Santo Domingo, 1983): 27.

48 Córdova, *Album del recuerdo*, 3 (Santo Domingo, 1981): 72.

49 Ibid., 42.

50 Ibid., 42.

51 As early as 1922, more than nineteen thousand fans paid more than 7,000 pesos to see the showdown between Licey and Escogido, of which almost 2,000 pesos went to the teams. Vicioso and Alvarez, *Béisbol dominicano*, 18.

52 Ibid., 16.

53 Donn Rogosin, *Invisible Men: Life in Baseball's Negro Leagues* (New York: Atheneum, 1985), 166.

54 Interview, Santo Domingo, 20 January 1989.

55 Ibid.

56 Rogosin, *Invisible Men*, 167.

57 Interview, Santo Domingo, 20 January 1989.

58 Rogosin, *Invisible Men*, 167.

59 Interview, Santo Domingo, 20 January 1989.

60 Interview (in Spanish), Santo Domingo, 16 January 1989.

61 Interview, Santo Domingo, 20 January 1989.

62 Vicioso and Alvarez, *Béisbol dominicano*, 20.

63 Córdova, *Album del recuerdo*, 1 (Santo Domingo, 1983): 61.

64 Cúqui Córdova, "Aguiles Martinez: electo campeón fielding en 'V de la Victoria' (1943)," *Listin diario* (Santo Domingo), 11 April 1987.

65 Ibid.

66 Interview, Santo Domingo, 20 January 1989.

67 Interview, New York, 31 July 1989.

68 Ibid.

69 Interview, New York, 25 June 1989.

70 Interview, New York, 24 June 1989.

71 Cúqui Córdova, "Aguiles Martínez: se destacó en serie interantillana de 1944," *Listin diario* (Santo Domingo), 25 April 1987.

72 Ibid.

73 Córdova, *Album del recuerdo*, 3: 57, 92, 98.

74 Heriberto Morrison, *Dominicanos en las grandes ligas* (Santo Domingo, 1987), 5.

75 Córdova, *Album del recuerdo*, 4: 27.

76 Interview, New York, 24 June 1989.

77 Ibid.

78 Ibid. "No scouts at all in the early '50s. They didn't even know we had good ballplayers down here."

79 Vicioso and Alvarez, *Béisbol dominicano*, 26.

80 Ibid., 25.

81 Interview, New York, 20 July 1989.

82 He played with the Allentown Dukes. *Listin diario*, 4 February 1989.

83 Córdova, *Album del recuerdo*, 3: 92.

84 Interview, New York, 5 August 1989.

85 Córdova, *Album del recuerdo*, 3:22.
86 Córdova, *Album del recuerdo*, 4:33.
87 Córdova, *Album del recuerdo*, 3:5.
88 Interview, New York, 5 August 1989.
89 Ibid.; Córdova, *Album del recuerdo*, 3:77.
90 Interview, New York, 24 June 1989.
91 Ibid.
92 Ibid.

CHAPTER TWO
The Political Economy of Dominican Baseball

1 Interview, Campo Las Palmas, 25 January 1989.
2 Working relationships are contracts between American major league teams and professional Dominican teams. They are more fully described in chapter 3.
3 Field interview, Campo Las Palmas, 28 December 1987.
4 Interview, Santo Domingo, 25 January 1989.
5 Interview, Santo Domingo, 13 April 1988.
6 Interview, Santo Domingo, 1 May 1988.
7 Interview, Santo Domingo, 13 April 1988.
8 Interview, Santo Domingo, 2 May 1988.
9 Interview, Santo Domingo, 12 December 1987.
10 Interview, Santo Domingo, 19 January 1989.
11 Field interview (in Spanish), Santo Domingo, 27 January 1989.
12 Field interview, Santo Domingo, 29 January 1989.
13 Alan M. Klein, "Houston Should Welcome Joaquin," *Houston Chronicle*, 1 April 1988.
14 *Listin diario*, 18 December 1987.
15 *Listin diario*, 24 January 1989.
16 Field interview, Campo Las Palmas, 4 January 1988.
17 Interview, Santo Domingo, 2 May 1988.
18 Interview, Santo Domingo, 29 January 1989.
19 Interview, Santo Domingo, 25 January 1989.
20 Field interview, Santo Domingo, 28 January 1989.
21 Field interview, Santo Domingo, 27 January 1989.
22 Field interview (in Spanish), Santo Domingo, 27 January 1989.
23 Interview, Santo Domingo, 25 January 1989.
24 Bill Brubaker, "Inside the Dominican Pipeline," *Washington Post*, 20 March 1986.
25 In 1985 the commissioner of Dominican baseball was appointed to oversee and arbitrate relations between American teams and Dominican players. By 1987 this appointment had been eliminated and, as of 1990, had not been filled.
26 Interview, Campo Las Palmas, 30 January 1989.

CHAPTER THREE
The Determinators

165

*Notes
to Pages
48–56*

1 *Listin diario*, 18 April 1988.

2 Interview, Santo Domingo, 25 January 1989.

3 Virtually every question I posed about amateur baseball provoked critical comments about corruption. On no other topic did my questions evince such widespread cynicism.

4 Interview, Campo Las Palmas, 21 December 1987.

5 Ralph Avila, director of the academy, says there are fifty-eight bilingual members of the Dodgers' staff, including coaches, managers, and scouts.

6 *Listin diario*, 25 January 1989. The pitcher is José Rijo, who has played for the New York Yankees, the Oakland Athletics, and the Cincinnati Reds.

7 *Listin diario*, 4 April 1988.

8 Field interview, Santo Domingo, 27 January 1989.

9 Ibid.

10 Field interview, Santo Domingo, 25 January 1989.

11 Field interview, Santo Domingo, 27 January 1989.

12 Interview, Santo Domingo, 12 April 1988.

13 Ibid.

14 Interview (in Spanish), Santo Domingo, 23 January 1989.

15 Field interview, Santo Domingo, 27 January 1989.

16 Field interview, Santo Domingo, 26 January 1989.

17 Field interview, Campo Las Palmas, 29 January 1989.

18 Interview, Santo Domingo, 29 January 1989.

19 Avila took the Japanese offer rather lightly, saying jokingly that it did not provide for enough money to pay his salary. Field interview, Campo Las Palmas, 16 January 1989.

20 Interview, Santo Domingo, 14 December 1987.

21 Interview, Santo Domingo, 20 April 1988.

22 Field interview, Santo Domingo, 21 January 1989.

23 Bill Brubaker, "Inside the Dominican Pipeline," *Washington Post*, 20 March 1986.

24 Ibid.

25 *Listin diario*, 22 January 1989.

26 Ibid.

27 Ibid.

28 Field interview (in Spanish), Santo Domingo, 23 January 1989.

29 Field interview, Santo Domingo, 15 January 1989.

30 Field interview, Santo Domingo, 28 January 1989.

31 Andre Gunder Frank, *Capitalism and Underdevelopment in Latin America* (New York: Monthly Review Press, 1969).

32 Frobel Folker, Jurgen Heinrichs, and Otto Kruge, *The New International Division of Labor* (Cambridge: Cambridge University Press, 1980); June Nash and Patricia Fernandez-Kelly, eds., *Women, Men, and the Inter-*

national Division of Labor (Albany: State University of New York Press, 1983).

33 George Pfister, of the office of the commissioner of baseball, quoted in Glen Macnow, "The Boys of Winter," *Detroit Free Press*, 4 February 1986.

34 Milton Jamail, "Hold On to the Dream: Latino Baseball Players in the U.S." (unpublished manuscript).

35 Richard Barnet and R. Muller, *Global Reach: Multinationals and the World Order* (New York: Simon and Schuster, 1976).

36 José Felipe Rivera, *Población y sociedad* (Santo Domingo, 1983), 327–29.

37 Brubaker, "Inside the Dominican Pipeline."

38 Harry Edwards, "The Collegiate Athletic Arms Race," *Journal of Sport and Social Issues* 8 (1984): 4–23.

39 *Baseball America*, 25 December 1989.

40 *New York Times*, 9 February 1988.

41 *Miami Herald*, 11 February 1990.

42 Interview, Santo Domingo, 28 April 1988; Milton Jamail, personal communication to author.

CHAPTER FOUR
The Wannabees

1 Bill Brubaker, "Caribbean Curve Ball: Baseball's Dominican Pipeline," *Washington Post National Weekly*, 31 March 1986.

2 *Toronto Globe and Mail*, 23 March 1989.

3 Interview, Santo Domingo, 24 April 1988.

4 Interview, Santo Domingo, 19 January 1989.

5 Interview, Santo Domingo, 4 April 1988.

6 Ibid.

7 Ibid.

8 Field notes, 26 January 1989.

9 Field interview (in Spanish), Santo Domingo, 28 April 1988.

10 Interview, Santo Domingo, 4 April 1988.

11 Interview (in Spanish), San Pedro de Macorís, 20 December 1987.

12 Interview, Santo Domingo, 4 April 1988.

13 Internal memorandum, Los Angeles Dodgers.

14 Arnold Van Gennep, *The Rites of Passage* (Chicago: University of Chicago Press, 1960); Gilbert Herdt, *The Gambia: Ritual and Gender in New Guinea* (Fort Worth: Holt, Rinehart, and Winston, 1987).

15 Ibid.

16 Interview (in Spanish), Campo Las Palmas, 28 April 1988.

17 Interview, Santo Domingo, 4 April 1988.

18 Interview (in Spanish), Campo Las Palmas, 3 February 1989.

19 Interview (in Spanish), Campo Las Palmas, 28 April 1988.

20 It seemed to me that pitchers were more apt than other players to be jealous of each other.

21 Interview (in Spanish), Santo Domingo, 2 February 1989.

22 Richard Lee, *The Dobe King* (Fort Worth: Holt, Rinehart, and Winston, 1987).

23 Field interview (in Spanish), Campo Las Palmas, 3 February 1989.

24 Field interview (in Spanish), Campo Las Palmas, 2 February 1989.

25 Field interview (in Spanish), San Pedro de Macorís, 22 April 1989.

26 Interview (in Spanish), Campo Las Palmas, 28 April 1988.

27 Field interview (in Spanish), Campo Las Palmas, 5 January 1988.

28 Field interview (in Spanish), Campo Las Palmas, 20 December 1987.

29 Field interview (in Spanish), Campo Las Palmas, 20 December 1987.

30 Interview (in Spanish), Campo Las Palmas, 5 January 1989.

31 Field interview (in Spanish), Campo Las Palmas, 5 January 1988.

32 Field interview (in Spanish), Campo Las Palmas, 6 January 1988.

33 Field interview (in Spanish), San Pedro de Macorís, 5 January 1988.

34 Field interview (in Spanish), Campo Las Palmas, 18 December 1987.

35 Interview, Santo Domingo, 24 April 1988.

36 Field interview (in Spanish), San Pedro de Macorís, 5 January 1988.

37 Field interview (in Spanish), Campo Las Palmas, 21 December 1987.

38 Interview, Santo Domingo, 28 April 1988.

39 Interview, Santo Domingo, 24 April 1988.

40 Field interview, Campo Las Palmas, 5 April 1988.

41 Interview, Santo Domingo, 4 April 1988.

42 Donn Rogosin, *Invisible Men: Life in Baseball's Negro Leagues* (New York: Atheneum, 1985).

43 Interview, Santo Domingo, 24 April 1988.

44 Interview, New York, 24 June 1989.

45 Field interview (in Spanish), Campo Las Palmas, 24 April 1988.

46 Field interview (in Spanish), Campo Las Palmas, 6 January 1988.

47 Field interview (in Spanish), Campo Las Palmas, 13 December 1987.

48 Field interview (in Spanish), Campo Las Palmas, 14 April 1988.

49 Glen Macnow, "The Boys of Winter," *Detroit Free Press*, 4 February 1986, sec. C, p. 8.

50 Field interview (in Spanish), Campo Las Palmas, 3 February 1989. That some Dominican players disappear into American cities after being released or demoted is also a factor behind the stricter visa policy of the U.S. Immigration and Naturalization Service.

51 By realistic dialogue I mean dialogue that is representative of the speaker's class and region, and typical of the social situation. For example, I took into account that a player is more likely to talk to service workers and police than to other types of people.

52 *Toronto Globe and Mail*, 23 March 1989.

53 Constanza Montana, "Latinball," *Chicago Tribune*, 23 August 1989.

54 Interview, Santo Domingo, 2 May 1988.

55 Hal Bodley, "Small Port City Is Hub of Dominican baseball," *USA Today*, 10 August 1989.

56 Montana, "Latinball."

57 Field interview, Campo Las Palmas, 8 April 1988. For more on labels as differential rewards see Irving Goffman, *Stigma: Notes on the Management of Social Identity* (New York: Touchstone, 1986); and Howard S. Becker, *Outsiders: Studies in the Sociology of Deviance* (New York: Free Press, 1966).

58 *Los Angeles Times*, 26 March 1990.

59 Ibid.

60 Milton Jamail, personal communication to author.

61 Jim Myers, "Beisbol: Everybody's Game," *USA Today*, 10 August 1989.

62 Horse-tail tea is an herbal remedy that is supposed to lower blood pressure.

63 Gilbert Joseph, "Forging the Regional Pastime: Baseball and Class in the Yucatan," *Sport and Society in Latin America*, ed. Joseph Arbena (Westport, Conn.: Greenwood, 1988): 29–62.

64 Interview, Santo Domingo, 27 December 1987.

65 Interview, Santo Domingo, 4 April 1988.

66 Ibid.

67 Ibid.

68 Ibid.

69 Ibid.

70 Ibid.

71 Ibid.

72 Field interview, Campo Las Palmas, 14 January 1989.

CHAPTER FIVE
Yo soy dominicano

1 Ariel Dorfman and Armand Mattelart, *How to Read Donald Duck* (New York: International General, 1975); Todd Gitlin, "Prime Time Ideology: The Hegemonic Process of Television," *Social Problems* 26 (1979): 251–66; D. Callimanopulos, "Film and the Third World," *Cultural Survival* 7 (1983): 24–27; Alan Wells, *Picture Tube Imperialism: The Impact of U.S. Television on Latin America* (Maryknoll, N.Y.: Orbis, 1972).

2 Antonio Gramsci, *Selections from Prison Notebooks* (London: Lawrence and Wisehart, 1971).

3 Raymond Williams, *Television, Technology, and Cultural Form* (New York: Schocken, 1977).

4 Hegemony has come to dominate discussions of film (see Jim Pines and Paul Wellemann, eds., *Questions of Third Cinema* [London: British Film Institute, 1987]; and the journal *Critical Studies in Mass Communication*), communications (see Gitlin, "Prime Time Ideology"; and Herbert Schiller, *Mass Communication and the American Empire* [Boston: Beacon Books, 1971]), and culture (see Herbert Gans, *Popular Culture and High Culture* [New York: Basic Books, 1974]; Ian Angus and Sut Jhally, eds., *Cultural Politics in Contemporary America* [New York: Routledge, 1989]; and the journal *Cultural Studies*).

5 Karl Marx and Friedrich Engels, *The German Ideology* (New York: International Publishers, 1971), 18.

6 James Scott, *Weapons of the Weak: Everyday Forms of Peasant Resistance* (New Haven and London: Yale University Press, 1983), 304.

7 Ibid.

8 Eugene Genovese, *Roll, Jordan, Roll: The World the Slaves Made* (New York: Vintage, 1974).

9 Scott, *Weapons of the Weak,* 320.

10 Expressions of ethnic and racial self-loathing can be found in North American society as well: in an effort to appear less ethnic some members of minority groups Americanize their names, undergo plastic surgery, and straighten or lighten their hair.

11 Frantz Fanon, *Black Skins, White Masks* (New York: Grove Press, 1967), 18.

12 C. L. R. James, *Beyond a Boundary* (New York: Pantheon, 1984), 38–39.

13 David Spitzer, "A Contemporary Political and Socio-economic History of Haiti and the Dominican Republic" (doctoral dissertation, University of California, Berkeley, 1976), 353–54.

14 Jan Kepper Black, *The Dominican Republic: Politics and Development in an Unsovereign State* (Boston: Allen and Unwin, 1986), 9.

15 Spitzer, "Contemporary Political and Socio-economic History," 350.

16 Howard J. Wiarda and Michael Kryzanek, *The Dominican Republic: A Caribbean Crucible* (Boulder: Westview, 1982), 30.

17 Black, *Dominican Republic,* 20.

18 Roger Plant, *Sugar and Modern Slavery: A Tale of Two Countries* (London: Zed Books, 1987); Fernando Cardoso and Enzo Faletto, *Dependency and Development in Latin America* (Berkeley: University of California Press, 1979).

19 Black, *Dominican Republic,* 53.

20 Ibid., 9.

21 Within the past decade basketball has grown in popularity in the larger urban areas like Santo Domingo and San Pedro de Macorís, where youngsters play the game in makeshift courts on the street.

22 [James Sullivan,] "Dispatch of American Minister to the Dominican Republic to Secretary of State Bryan, 1 November 1913, No. 13" (Washington: National Archives, Department of State Records).

23 Anthony Wallace, *Death and Rebirth of the Seneca* (New York: Van Nostrand Reinhold, 1970); James Mooney, *Ghost Dance Religion and the Sioux Outbreak of 1890,* Bureau of American Ethnology, 14th Annual Report (Washington, 1896).

24 Anthony Wallace, *Modal Personality Structure of the Tuscarora Indians,* Bureau of American Ethnology, Bulletin 150 (Washington, 1952).

25 Edward Dozier, *The Pueblos of North America* (New York: Holt, Rinehart, and Winston, 1970).

26 Susan Eckstein, ed., *Power and Popular Protest* (Berkeley: University of California Press, 1989).

27 Scott, *Weapons of the Weak.*

28 Dick Hebdige, *Subculture: The Meaning of Style* (London: Methuen, 1983).

29 June Nash, "Cultural Resistance and Class Consciousness in Bolivian Tin Mining Communities," *Power and Popular Protest,* ed. Susan Eckstein (Berkeley: University of California Press, 1989): 182–203.

30 Raymond Williams, *Marxism and Literature* (New York: Oxford University Press, 1977).

31 Eric Wolf, *Peasant Wars of the Twentieth Century* (New York: Harper and Row, 1972); E. J. Hobsbawm, *Primitive Rebels* (New York: W. W. Norton, 1972).

32 Genovese, *Roll, Jordan, Roll,* 596.

33 Max Gluckman, *Order and Rebellion in Tribal Africa* (London: Cohen, 1969).

34 Terry Eagleton, quoted in *Toward a Revolutionary Criticism,* ed. Walter Benjamin (London: Verso, 1971), 148.

35 Gerald Mullin, *Flight and Rebellion: Slave Resistance in 18th Century Virginia* (New York: Oxford University Press, 1972).

36 Genovese, *Roll, Jordan, Roll,* 599–612.

37 *Cultural Survival* 7 (1983); Ariel Dorfman, *The Empire's New Clothes* (New York: Pantheon, 1983).

38 Herbert Gans, *The Urban Villagers: Group and Class in the Life of Italian-Americans* (New York: Glencoe, 1969).

39 Christine Gailey, "Rambo in Tonga: Video Film and Cultural Resistance in Tonga," *Culture* 9 (1990): 20–33.

40 Michael Miner (screenwriter for the film *Robocop*), personal communication to author.

41 George Mosse, ed., *Nazi Culture* (New York: Schocken, 1981).

42 Dorfman, *Empire's New Clothes.*

43 Wiarda and Kryzanek, *Dominican Republic,* 19.

44 I am deeply indebted for the ideas expressed in this section to Bruce Calder, *The Impact of Intervention: The Dominican Republic during the U.S. Intervention of 1916–1924* (Austin: University of Texas Press, 1984).

45 Spitzer, "Contemporary Political and Socio-economic History," 350.

46 Calder, *Impact of Intervention,* xvii.

47 Paul Muto, "The Illusory Promise: The Dominican Republic and the Process of Economic Development, 1900–1930 (doctoral dissertation, University of Washington, Seattle, 1976), 155.

48 Calder, *Impact of Intervention,* 241.

49 Ibid., 241.

50 Ibid., 195.

51 Vicioso and Alvarez, *Béisbol dominicano,* 16.

52 Truly poor people no longer attend games, especially since the cost of tickets has gone up. Nevertheless, those who cannot attend baseball games still manage to follow the sport on radio and television and in the newspapers.

53 Thomas E. Weil et al., *The Dominican Republic: A Country Study* (Washington: U.S. Government Printing Office, 1982), 35.

54 Wiarda and Kryzanek, *Dominican Republic*, 45–90.

55 Most countries highlight their own sports, but in the Dominican Republic and Japan it is acknowledged that the United States is preeminent at baseball. The American press reports on baseball elsewhere with less respect. By ignoring the curious baseball played at odd times of the year in Latin America, the spring baseball issue of *Sports Illustrated* unwittingly fosters the impression that the baseball season only "really" begins in the spring.

56 *Sports Illustrated*, 18 May 1987, pp. 27–28; *Boston Globe*, 17 July 1988, sec. C, p. 1.

57 *Sports Illustrated*, 18 May 1987.

58 *Listin diario*, 29 December 1987.

59 *Listin diario*, 10 April 1988.

60 *Listin diario*, 17 April 1988.

61 *Listin diario*, 20 April 1988.

62 Christopher Lasch, *The Culture of Narcissism* (New York: W. W. Norton, 1979).

63 *Listin diario*, 10 April 1988.

64 *Ultima hora*, 30 May 1987. The article incorrectly refers to twenty-four teams rather than twenty-six.

65 *Listin diario*, 18 April 1988.

66 *Listin diario*, 22 April 1988.

67 *Listin diario*, 14 April 1988. The subtotals add up to eighteen, not the nineteen to which the story refers.

68 *Listin diario*, 31 January 1989.

69 *Listin diario*, 24 January 1989.

70 *Listin diario*, 24 January 1989.

71 *Listin diario*, 26 January 1989.

72 Field interview, 28 January 1989.

73 *Listin diario*, 27 January 1989.

74 *Toronto Globe and Mail*, 23 March 1989.

75 Ibid.

76 The Blue Jays have had problems precisely because they have not set up an infrastructure in their minor league system (for example in Knoxville, Tennessee) to develop their players culturally and psychologically.

77 *Toronto Globe and Mail*, 23 March 1989.

78 George Bell, quoted in *Toronto Globe and Mail*, 23 March 1989.

79 *Toronto Globe and Mail*, 23 March 1989.

CHAPTER SIX
Quisqueya Qulture

1 Alejandro Portes, Manuel Castells, and Lauren Benton, eds., *The Informal Economy: Studies in Advanced and Less Developed Countries* (Baltimore: Johns Hopkins University Press, 1989).

2. Manuel Castells and Alejandro Portes, "World Underneath: The Origins, Dynamics and Effects of the Informal Economy," *The Informal Economy*, ed. Portes, Castells, and Benton, 11.

3 José Blanes Jiménez, "Cocaine, Informality, and the Urban Economy in La Paz, Bolivia," *The Informal Economy*, ed. Portes, Castells, and Benton, 135–50.

4 Field notes, 29 December 1987.

5 Brent Staples, "Where Are the Black Fans?" *New York Times Magazine*, 17 May 1987; *USA Today*, 5 June 1990.

6 Field notes, 24 January 1989.

7 Field notes, 25 January 1989.

8 Many journalists have written accounts of Dominican baseball. Some, such as John Krich's book *El béisbol* (New York: Random House, 1989), offer studied insights into aspects of the culture. Others, such as Macnow, "The Boys of Winter," *Detroit Free Press*, 4 February 1986, and Bill Brubaker, "Inside the Dominican Pipeline," *Washington Post*, 20 March 1986, probe such specific issues as the difficulties encountered by Dominican rookies in the United States.

9 The flip game is played by two or more players who tap the ball to each other. The first to let the ball hit the ground loses.

10 Field interview, Santo Domingo, 23 April 1988.

11 Even though Escogido has a following of fans from every stratum, it is known as the team of the affluent Dominicans.

12 One former major leaguer who had managed in the Dominican league wanted no part of it any longer. He told me stories of players who ignored all his admonishments, of an American player who was instructed by his American manager to learn bunting from him but who failed to show up for his lessons because he was busy playing golf, and of other players who did not show up for games because they said they were ill and yet at night went dancing.

13 Field interview, Santo Domingo, 23 January 1989.

14 Field interview, Santo Domingo, 30 January 1989.

15 Victor Turner, *The Anthropology of Performance* (New York: PAJ Publications, 1987).

CHAPTER SEVEN
Sugarball

1 David Spitzer, "A Contemporary Political and Socio-economic History of Haiti and the Dominican Republic" (doctoral dissertation, University of California, Berkeley, 1976), 350.

2 John Hargreaves, "Sport, Culture, and Ideology," *Sport, Culture, and Ideology*, ed. Jennifer Hargreaves (London: Routledge and Kegan Paul, 1982), 30–61; Ian Taylor, "Class, Violence, and Sport: The Case of Soccer Hooliganism In Britain," *Sport, Culture, and the Modern State*, ed.

H. Cantelon and R. Gruneau (Toronto: University of Toronto Press,
1982), 39–96; Peter Donnelly, "Sport as a Site for 'Popular Resistance,'"
Popular Cultures and Political Practices, ed. R. Gruneau (Toronto: Gara-
mond Press, 1988).

3 Hargreaves, "Sport, Culture, and Ideology," 52.
4 Elliott Gorn, *The Manly Art: Bare Knuckle Fighting in America* (Ithaca:
Cornell University Press, 1986); Matthew Shirts, "Socrates, Corinthians,
and Questions of Democracy and Citizenship," *Sport and Society in Latin
America*, ed. Joseph Arbena (Westport, Conn.: Greenwood, 1988),
97–113.
5 *Trobriand Cricket* (documentary film).
6 Donald Rhoden, "Baseball and the Quest for National Identity in Meiji
Japan," *American Historical Review* 85 (1980): 511–34.
7 Ibid., 521
8 Gilbert Joseph, "Forging the Regional Pastime: Class and Baseball in Yucatán," *Sport and Society in Latin America*, ed. Joseph Arbana (Westview,
Conn.: Greenwood, 1988): 29–62.
9 Ibid., 33.
10 Ibid., 38.
11 David LaFrance, "A Mexican Popular Image of the United States through
the Baseball Hero, Fernando Valenzuela," *Studies in Latin American
Popular Culture* 4 (1985): 14–22.
12 Ibid., 20.
13 Jay Mandle and Joan Mandle, *Grass Roots Commitment: Basketball and
Society in Trinidad and Tobago* (Parkersburg, Iowa: Caribbean Books,
1988).
14 C. L. R. James, *Beyond a Boundary* (New York: Pantheon, 1984).
15 Claude Lévi-Strauss, *Structural Anthropology* (New York: Basic Books,
1972).
16 Dick Hebdige, *Subculture: The Meaning of Style* (London: Methuen,
1983).
17 J. Clark, "Style," *Resistance through Ritual*, ed. Stewart Hall and T.
Jefferson (London: Hutchison University Library, 1983), 56–89.
18 Bertolt Brecht, quoted in Ernst Becker, *The Necessity of Art* (London: Per-
egrin, 1978), 10.
19 Walter Benjamin, "The Work of Art in the Age of Mechanical Reproduc-
tion," *Illuminations* (New York: Schocken, 1969), 221–87.

Index